PHILIP'S

FAMILY WORLD ATLAS

PHILIP'S

FAMILY
WORLD
ATLAS

CONTENTS

1 **General Reference**
  The World: Physical
2 **The World: Political**
4 **Europe**
5 **British Isles** 1:4M
6 **England and Wales** 1:2M
8 **Scotland** 1:2M
9 **Ireland** 1:2M
10 **Central Europe** 1:5M
12 **France** 1:5M
13 **Spain and Portugal** 1:5M
14 **Italy and the Balkan States** 1:5M
16 **Scandinavia and the
  Baltic Lands** 1:5M
18 **Russia and Central Asia** 1:20M
20 **Asia** 1:50M
21 **South-west Asia** 1:20M
22 **Southern Asia** 1:20M
23 **South-east Asia** 1:20M
24 **Japan** 1:10M
  Southern Japan 1:5M
25 **China** 1:20M
26 **Australia** 1:12M
  Australia: Physical 1:80M

28 **New Zealand** 1:6M
  **New Zealand and
  South-west Pacific** 1:60M
  **Fiji and Tonga Islands,
  Samoa Islands** 1:12M
29 **Africa** 1:40M
30 **Northern Africa** 1:15M
32 **Central and Southern
  Africa** 1:15M
34 **Canada** 1:15M
  Alaska 1:30M
36 **United States** 1:12M
  Hawaii 1:10M
38 **Mexico** 1:12M
  Panama Canal 1:1M
39 **West Indies** 1:12M
  Bermuda 1:1M
  **Leeward Islands,
  Windward Islands,
  Jamaica , Trinidad and
  Tobago** 1:8M
40 **South America – North** 1:16M
42 **South America – South** 1:16M
43 **Index**

Published by George Philip Limited
59 Grosvenor Street, London W1X 9DA

ISBN 0 540 05680 4

© 1992 George Philip Limited

Edited by B.M. Willett

Printed in Hong Kong

I

GENERAL REFERENCE

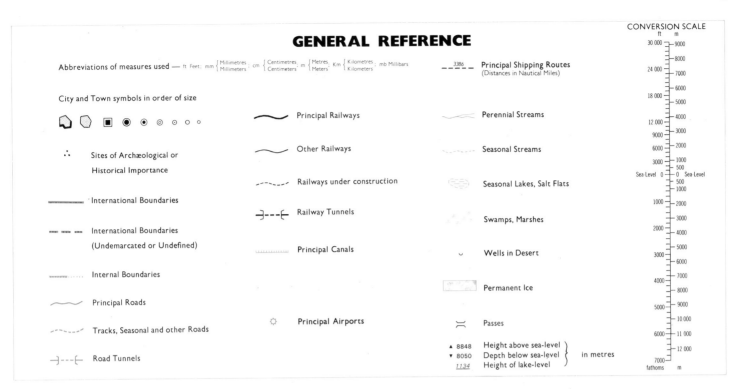

Abbreviations of measures used — ft Feet; mm {Millimetres / Millimeters} cm {Centimetres / Centimeters} m {Metres / Meters} Km {Kilometres / Kilometers} mb Millibars

City and Town symbols in order of size

∴ Sites of Archæological or Historical Importance

International Boundaries

International Boundaries (Undemarcated or Undefined)

Internal Boundaries

Principal Roads

Tracks, Seasonal and other Roads

Road Tunnels

Principal Railways

Other Railways

Railways under construction

Railway Tunnels

Principal Canals

Principal Airports

3386 Principal Shipping Routes (Distances in Nautical Miles)

Perennial Streams

Seasonal Streams

Seasonal Lakes, Salt Flats

Swamps, Marshes

Wells in Desert

Permanent Ice

Passes

▲ 8848 Height above sea-level
▼ 8050 Depth below sea-level } in metres
1134 Height of lake-level

CONVERSION SCALE

THE WORLD
Physical
1:150 000 000

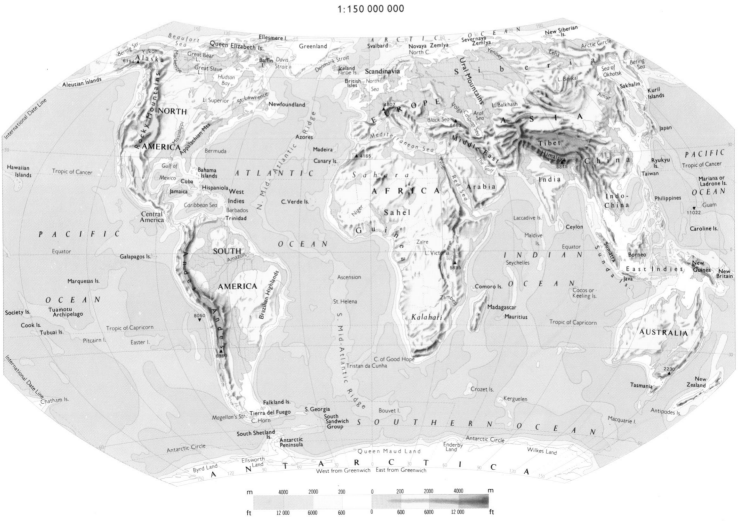

Projection: Hammer Equal Area

COPYRIGHT. GEORGE PHILIP & SON. LTD.

Projection: Hammer Equal Area

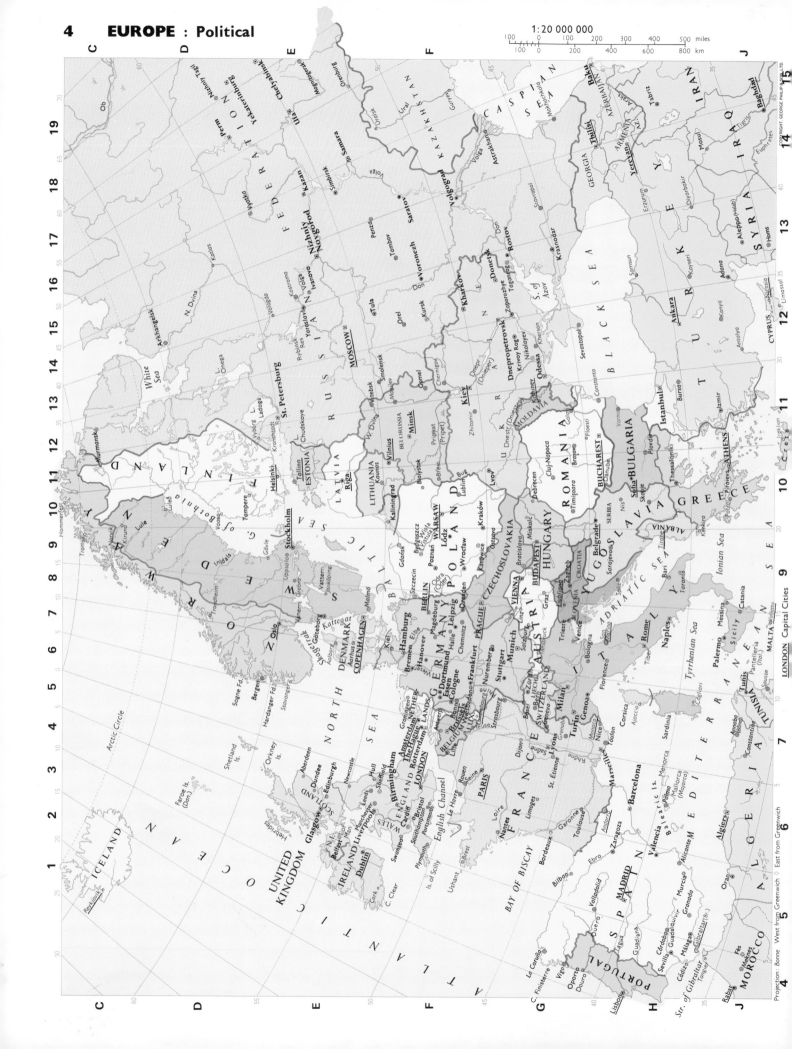

1 : 4 000 000

20   0   20   40   60 miles
20   0   20   40   60   80
                              km

The DISTRICTS of Northern Ireland have been numbered
and can be identified by reference to this table.

1 Londonderry	14 Craigavon
2 Limavady	15 Armagh
3 Coleraine	16 Newry & Mourne
4 Ballymoney	17 Banbridge
5 Moyle	18 Down
6 Larne	19 Lisburn
7 Ballymena	20 Antrim
8 Magherafelt	21 Newtownabbey
9 Cookstown	22 Carrickfergus
10 Strabane	23 North Down
11 Omagh	24 Ards
12 Fermanagh	25 Castlereagh
13 Dungannon	26 Belfast

ORKNEY

Kirkwall

HIGHLAND

SHETLAND

Lerwick

WESTERN
ISLES

Stornoway

HIGHLAND GRAMPIAN

Inverness

SCOTLAND

Aberdeen

TAYSIDE

Dundee

FIFE
Glenrothes

CENTRAL
Stirling

Edinburgh
LOTHIAN

ATLANTIC

STRATHCLYDE

Glasgow

Newtown
St. Boswells

BORDERS

NORTH
SEA

OCEAN

DUMFRIES
AND
GALLOWAY

Dumfries

NORTHUMBERLAND
Morpeth

Newcastle
TYNE AND
WEAR

North Channel

Carlisle

Durham

DONEGAL
Lifford

Londonderry

NORTHERN
IRELAND

T y r o n e

Fermanagh

Antrim

Belfast

Down

CUMBRIA

DURHAM

CLEVELAND
Middlesbrough

Northallerton

ISLE OF
MAN

Douglas

NORTH
YORKSHIRE

Sligo

SLIGO

LEITRIM

Monaghan

MONAGHAN

Armagh

Carrick-on-
Shannon

Cavan

Dundalk

MAYO
Castlebar

CAVAN

LOUTH

IRISH SEA

LANCASHIRE
Preston

HUMBERSIDE
Beverley

WEST
YORKSHIRE
Wakefield

ROSCOMMON

Roscommon

Longford
LONGFORD

Mullingar
WESTMEATH

An Uaimh
(Navan)

MEATH

GREATER
MANCHESTER

MERSEYSIDE Manchester
Liverpool

Barnsley
SOUTH
YORKSHIRE

ENGLAND

Lincoln

GALWAY
Galway

OFFALY

DUBLIN
Dublin

Chester
CHESHIRE

DERBYSHIRE

Matlock

NOTT-
INGHAM-
SHIRE

LINCOLNSHIRE

Tullamore

KILDARE

Naas

Caernarfon

Mold

IRELAND

Port Laoise

CLWYD

Nottingham

LAOIS

Wicklow

GWYNEDD

Stafford
STAFFORD-
SHIRE

Leicester

NORFOLK
Norwich

CLARE
Ennis

Carlow
CARLOW

WICKLOW

Shrewsbury

SHROPSHIRE

LEICESTERSHIRE

Kilkenny

Limerick

TIPPERARY

KILKENNY

WEST
MIDLANDS
Birmingham

WARWICK-
SHIRE
Warwick

NORTH-
AMPTON-
SHIRE
Northampton

CAMBRIDGE-
SHIRE

SUFFOLK

LIMERICK

WEXFORD

WALES

POWYS

HEREFORD
AND
WORCESTER

Worcester

Bedford
BEDFORD-
SHIRE

Cambridge

Ipswich

Tralee

Clonmel

WATERFORD

Wexford

Llandrindod
Wells

BUCK-
INGHAM-
SHIRE

Hertford
HERTFORD-
SHIRE

ESSEX
Chelmsford

KERRY

Waterford

DYFED

Carmarthen

Gloucester
GLOUCESTER-
SHIRE

Oxford
OXFORDSHIRE

Aylesbury

GREATER
LONDON

CORK

Cork

St. George's Channel

WEST
GLAMORGAN
Swansea

GWENT
Cwmbran

MID
GLAMORGAN

Cardiff

SOUTH
GLAMORGAN

Bristol

AVON

BERKSHIRE

Reading

Kingston

Maidstone

WILTSHIRE
Trowbridge

SURREY

KENT

CELTIC

SOMERSET

HAMPSHIRE
Winchester

WEST
SUSSEX

EAST
SUSSEX
Lewes

SEA

Taunton

Chichester

DEVON

DORSET
Dorchester

Newport
ISLE OF
WIGHT

Exeter

CORNWALL

ENGLISH   CHANNEL

Truro

FRANCE

○ Norwich   Administrative headquarters
MERSEYSIDE   Metropolitan counties
Antrim   Former Northern Ireland
                counties

Projection: *Conical with two standard parallels*

West from Greenwich 0 East from Greenwich
COPYRIGHT. GEORGE PHILIP & SON. LTD.

NORTH SEA

IRISH SEA

North Channel

SCOTLAND

ENGLAND

WALES

Southern Uplands

Cheviot Hills

CUMBRIA

Cumbrian Mts.

NORTHUMBERLAND

DURHAM

CLEVELAND

TYNE & WEAR

N. YORK MOORS

NORTH YORKSHIRE

WEST YORKSHIRE

SOUTH YORKSHIRE

HUMBERSIDE

LINCOLN

LANCASHIRE

MERSEYSIDE

GREATER MANCHESTER

CHESHIRE

DERBY

NOTT

STAFFORD

CLWYD

GWYNEDD

Pennine

Galloway

Kintyre

ISLE OF MAN

Anglesey

Holderness

Lincoln Wold

Forest of Bowland

Inveraray
Crinan
Cairn
Lochgilphead
B. Lomond 974
L. Katrine
Trossachs
L. Lomond
Forth
Stirling
Ochil Hills
Alloa
L. Leven
Kinross
L. Leven
Dunfermline
Falkirk
Linlithgow
Airdrie
Coatbridge
Glasgow
Clydebank
Dumbarton
Rutherglen
Hamilton
Motherwell
Wishaw
Paisley
Port Glasgow
Greenock
Helensburgh
Dunoon
Largs
Saltcoats
Irvine
Kilmarnock
Ayr
Prestwick
Goat Fell 874
Arran
Campbeltown
Mull of Kintyre
Ailsa Craig
Girvan
Ayr
Doon
Sanquhar
Nith
Dumfries
Leadhills
Lanark
Carstairs
Peebles
Moorfoot Hills
Pentland Hills
Edinburgh
Leith
Musselburgh
Haddington
Dunbar
North Berwick
Bass Rock
St. Abb's Hd.
Eyemouth
Coldstream
Tweed
Kelso
Jedburgh
Galashiels
Selkirk
Hawick
Lammermuir Hills
Berwick-upon-Tweed
Holy I.
Farne Is.
Alnwick
Coquet
Flodden
Till
The Cheviot 816
Morpeth
Ashington
Blyth
Newcastle
Tynemouth
Wallsend
South Shields
Gateshead
Sunderland
Houghton-le-Spring
Consett
Durham
Blaydon
Hexham
N. Tyne
S. Tyne
HADRIAN'S WALL
Haltwhistle
Alston
Cross Fell 893
Penrith
Appleby
Brough
Eden
Carlisle
Gretna Green
Annan
Langholm
Longtown
Dalbeattie
Castle Douglas
Kirkcudbright
Newton Stewart
Wigtown
Stranraer
Portpatrick
Whithorn
Wigtown Bay
Luce Bay
Mull of Galloway
Solway Firth
Maryport
Workington
Whitehaven
St. Bee's Hd.
Seascale
Derwent
Keswick
Skiddaw 931
Helvellyn 960
Derwentwater
Ullswater
Ambleside
Windermere
Kendal
Sca Fell 978
Millom
Ulverston
Barrow
Walney I.
Morecambe Bay
Fleetwood
Cleveleys
Blackpool
Lytham-St. Annes
Southport
Formby Pt.
Ormskirk
Bootle
Wallasey
Birkenhead
Liverpool
St. Helens
Widnes
Runcorn
Ellesmere Port
Chester
Wrexham
Mold
Flint
Rhyl
Colwyn Bay
Llandudno
Gt. Ormes Hd.
Conway
Bangor
Beaumaris
Amlwch
Holyhead
Holy I.
Caernarfon
Menai Strait
Snowdon 1085
Portmadoc
Ffestiniog
Harlech
Pwllheli
Nefyn
Braich-y-Pwll
Lancaster
Heysham
Preston
Chorley
Blackburn
Accrington
Burnley
Nelson
Colne
Bolton
Bury
Rochdale
Oldham
Manchester
Salford
Stockport
Warrington
Northwich
Crewe
Nantwich
Whitchurch
Macclesfield
Buxton
Leek
Stoke-on-Trent
Newcastle-under-Lyme
Uttoxeter
Burton
Derby
Ilkeston
Heanor
Belper
Matlock
Chesterfield
Sheffield
Rotherham
Barnsley
Wakefield
Huddersfield
Halifax
Bradford
Leeds
Harrogate
Knaresborough
Ripon
Skipton
Settle
Ingleborough
Whernside
Pen-y-Ghent 693
Gt. Whernside 704
Wensleydale
Swaledale
Richmond
Northallerton
Thirsk
Darlington
Bishop Auckland
Barnard Castle
Stockton
Middlesbrough
Billingham
Hartlepool
Redcar
Saltburn
Whitby
Scarborough
Filey
Flamborough Hd.
Bridlington
Driffield
Beverley
Hull
Withernsea
Hornsea
Spurn Hd.
Immingham
Grimsby
Cleethorpes
Scunthorpe
Goole
Selby
Doncaster
Pontefract
Castleford
Gainsborough
Market Rasen
Louth
Mablethorpe
Alford
Skegness
Horncastle
Lincoln
Newark
Retford
Worksop
Mansfield
Sutton-in-Ashfield
Nottingham
Beeston
Long Eaton
Boston
Sleaford
Grantham
The Wash
Cromer
North Walsham
Fakenham
Hunstanton
Wells
Sandringham
York
Ure
Nidd
Wharfe
Ouse
Trent
Witham
Derwent
Rye
Pickering
Malton
Esk
Tees
Wear
Eden
Lune
Ribble
Dee
Mersey
Weaver
Don
Aire
Calder

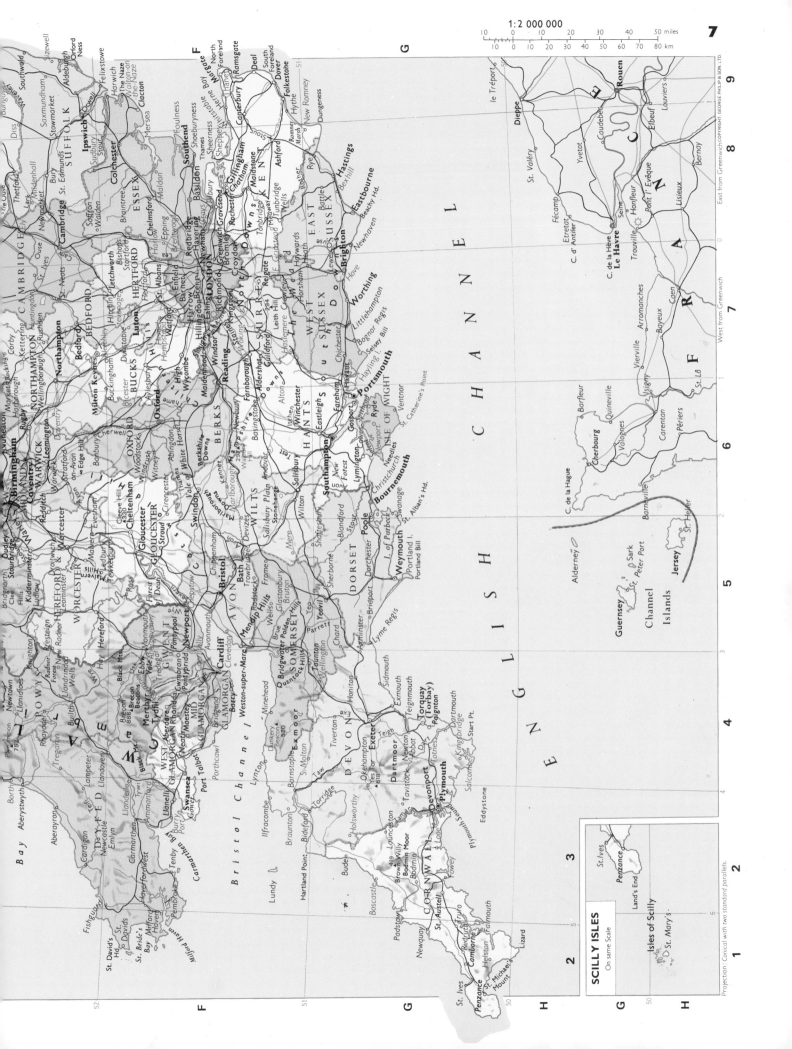

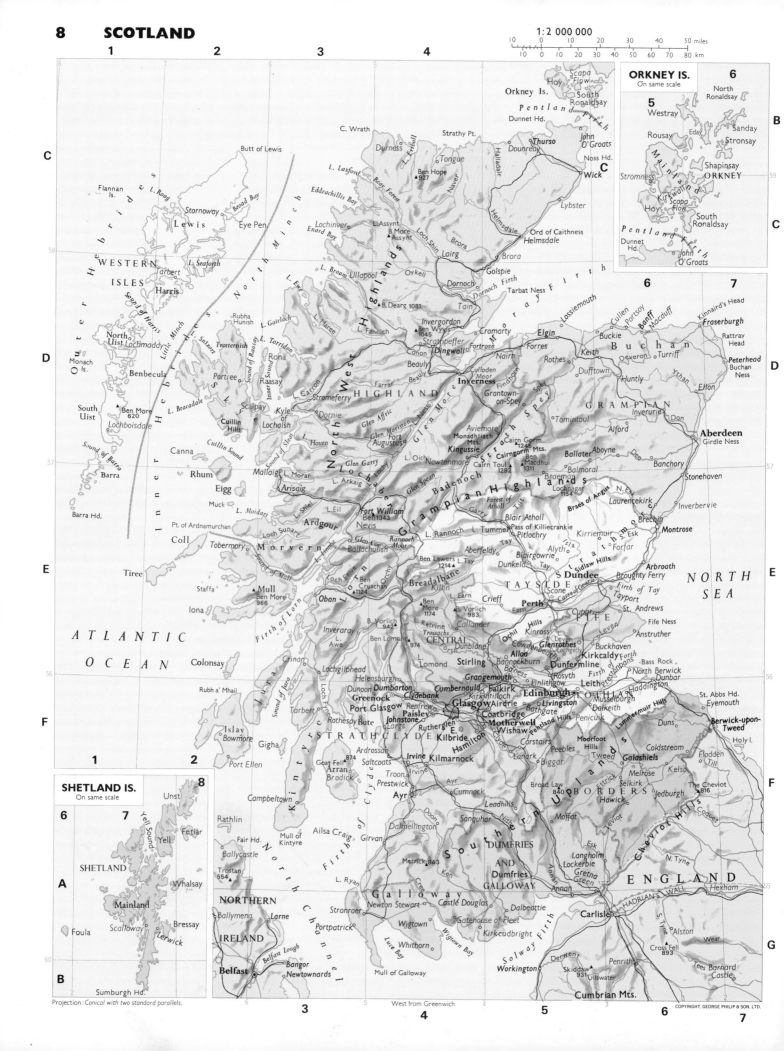

1:2 000 000

ORKNEY IS.
On same scale

SHETLAND IS.
On same scale

Projection: Conical with two standard parallels.

West from Greenwich

COPYRIGHT. GEORGE PHILIP & SON. LTD.

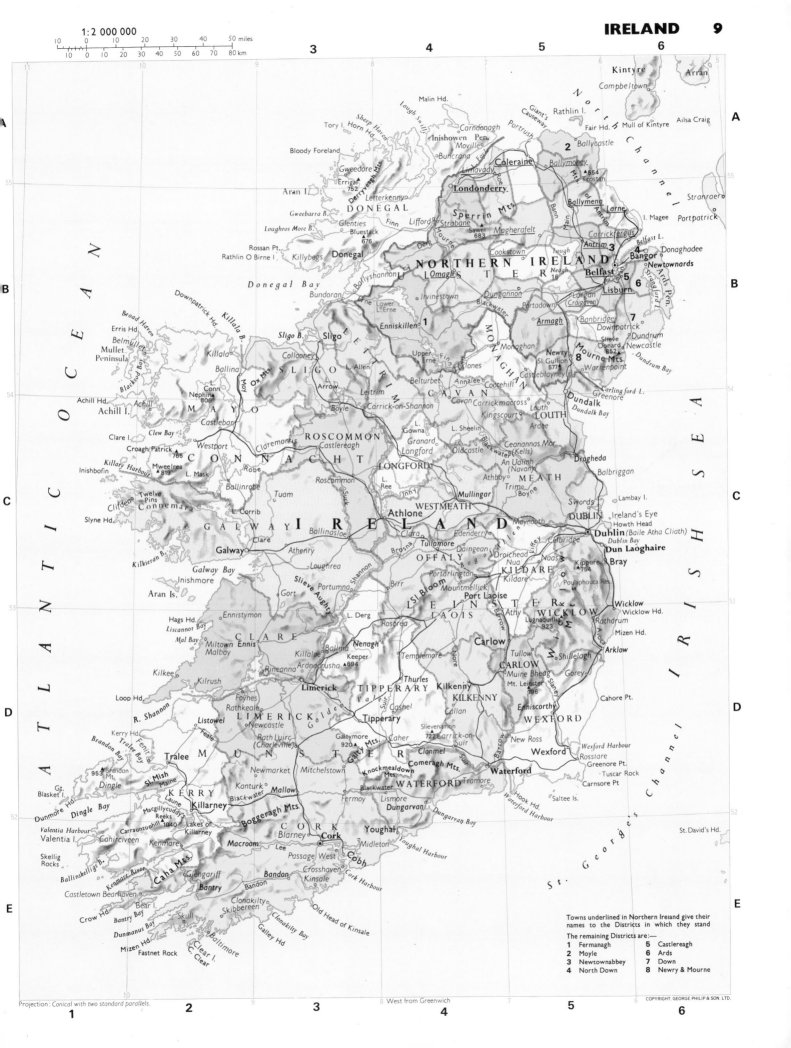

1 : 2 000 000

10   0   10   20   30   40   50 miles
10   0   10 20 30 40 50 60 70 80 km

Towns underlined in Northern Ireland give their
names to the Districts in which they stand

The remaining Districts are:—

1 Fermanagh	5	Castlereagh
2 Moyle	6	Ards
3 Newtownabbey	7	Down
4 North Down	8	Newry & Mourne

Projection: Conical with two standard parallels.

West from Greenwich

COPYRIGHT. GEORGE PHILIP & SON. LTD.

East from Greenwich

1:5 000 000

| 40 20 0 | 20 10 0 | 20 | 40 | 60 | 80 | 100 miles |
| 40 | 20 0 | 40 | 80 | 120 | 160 km |

FRENCH DEPARTMENTS

Abbr.	No.	Department
A.	01	Ain
Ai.	02	Aisne
Al.	03	Allier
A.H.P.	04	Alpes-de-Haute-Provence
H.A.	05	Hautes-Alpes
A.M.	06	Alpes-Maritimes
Ard.	07	Ardèche
Ar.	08	Ardennes
Ar.	09	Ariège
Aub.	10	Aube
Aud.	11	Aude
Av.	12	Aveyron
B.Rh.	13	Bouches-du-Rhône
Ca.	14	Calvados
Ch.	15	Cantal
Ch.	16	Charente
Ch.M.	17	Charente-Maritime
Che.	18	Cher
	19	Corrèze
C.O.	20	Corse a) Haute-Corse b) Corse du Sud
	21	Côte-d'Or
C.A.	22	Côtes d'Armor
Cr.	23	Creuse
D.	24	Dordogne
Do.	25	Doubs
Dr.	26	Drôme
E.	27	Eure
E.L.	28	Eure-et-Loir
F.	29	Finistère
G.	30	Gard
H.G.	31	Haute-Garonne
Ge.	32	Gers
Gi.	33	Gironde
H.	34	Hérault
I.V.	35	Ille-et-Vilaine
I.	36	Indre
I.L.	37	Indre-et-Loire
Is.	38	Isère
J.	39	Jura
La.	40	Landes
L.C.	41	Loir-et-Cher
Lo.	42	Loire
H.L.	43	Haute-Loire
L.A.	44	Loire-Atlantique
Loi.	45	Loiret
Lot	46	Lot
L.G.	47	Lot-et-Garonne
Loz.	48	Lozère
M.L.	49	Maine-et-Loire
M.	50	Manche
Ma.	51	Marne
H.M.	52	Haute-Marne
May.	53	Mayenne
M.M.	54	Meurthe-et-Moselle
Me.	55	Meuse
Mo.	56	Morbihan
Mos.	57	Moselle
N.	58	Nièvre
No.	59	Nord
O.	60	Oise
Or.	61	Orne
P.D.	62	Pas-de-Calais
P.D.	63	Puy-de-Dôme
P.A.	64	Pyrénées-Atlantiques
H.P.	65	Hautes-Pyrénées
P.O.	66	Pyrénées-Orientales
B.Rh.	67	Bas-Rhin
H.R.	68	Haut-Rhin
Rh.	69	Rhône
H.S.	70	Haute-Saône
S.L.	71	Saône-et-Loire
Sa.	72	Sarthe
Sa.	73	Savoie
H.Sa.	74	Haute-Savoie
	75	Paris
S.Me.	76	Seine-Maritime
S.M.	77	Seine-et-Marne
Y.	78	Yvelines
D.S.	79	Deux-Sèvres
So.	80	Somme
T.	81	Tarn
T.G.	82	Tarn-et-Garonne
Va.	83	Var
Va.	84	Vaucluse
V.	85	Vendée
Vi.	86	Vienne
H.V.	87	Haute-Vienne
Vo.	88	Vosges
Y.	89	Yonne
B.	90	Belfort
Es.	91	Essonne
H.Se.	92	Hauts-de-Seine
S.S.D.	93	Seine-St-Denis
V.M.	94	Val-de-Marne
V.O.	95	Val-d'Oise

CORSICA
On same scale

(Corse — Haute-Corse, Corse du Sud; Mte. Rotondo 2625; Bastia, Calvi, Ajaccio, Bonifacio, Porto-Vecchio)

MEDITERRANEAN SEA

BAY OF BISCAY

ENGLISH CHANNEL

GERMANY · BELGIUM · LUXEMBOURG · SWITZERLAND · ITALY · ANDORRA · SPAIN

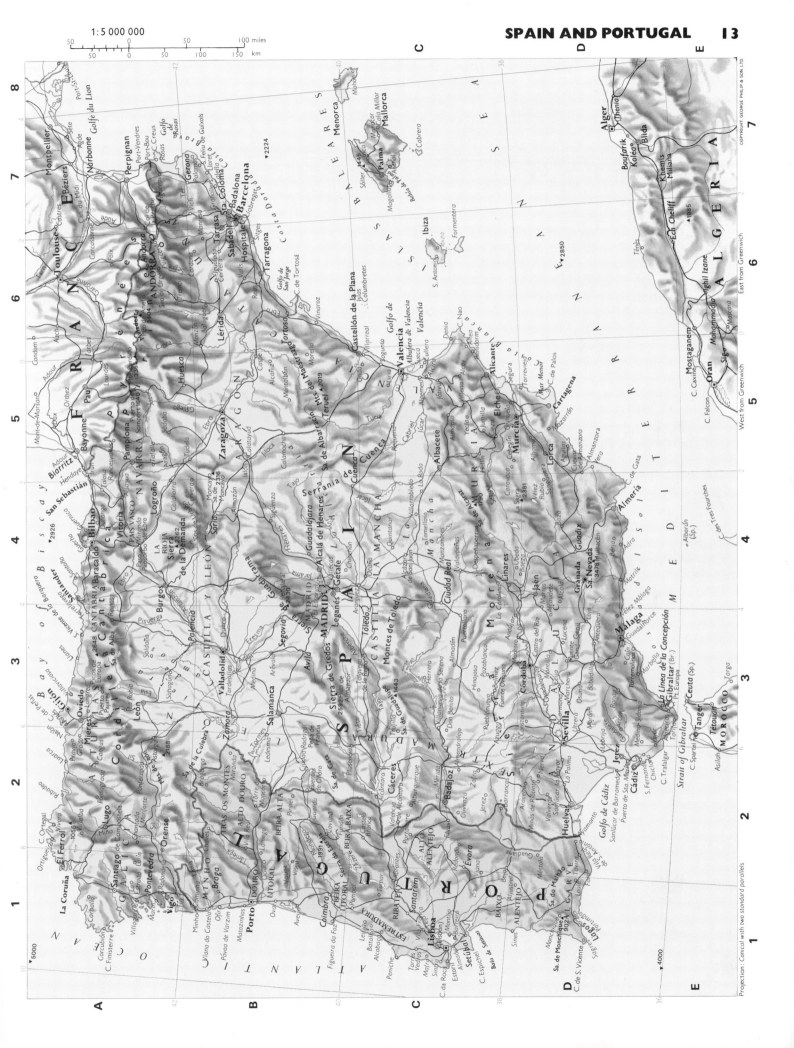

1:5 000 000

50   50   0   50   100 miles
50   0   50   100   150 km

East from Greenwich

West from Greenwich

Projection: Conical with two standard parallels

ICELAND
on the same scale
as general map

NORWEGIAN SEA

FINNMARK

LAPPI

OULU

VAASA

TROMS

NORRBOTTEN

VÄSTERBOTTEN

JÄMTLAND

N-TRØNDELAG

SØR-TRØNDELAG

MØRE

Vadsø · Vardø · Tanafjorden · Nikel · Kirkenes · Kiberg

Lakselfjorden · Porsangen · Nordkapp · Honningsvåg · Hammerfest · Alta · Kautokeino

Lopphavet · Kvænangen · Sørøya · Sørkjosen · Skibotn

Tromsø · Senja · Narvik · Ofoten · Tysfjord · Bardu

Andøy · Hinnøy · Vesterålen · Langøya · Austvågøy

Lofoten · Vestvågøy · Moskenstraumen · Værøy · Røst

Bodø · Saltfjell · Mo · Mosjøen · Brønnøysund · Vega

Namsos · Steinkjer · Levanger · Trondheim · Orkanger

Kristiansund · Molde · Ålesund · Stadlandet

Kiruna · Gällivare · Malmberget · Jokkmokk · Boden · Luleå

Piteå · Skellefteå · Umeå · Örnsköldsvik · Härnösand · Sollefteå

Östersund · Storsjön

Oulu · Kemi · Tornio · Haparanda · Kalix · Kokkola (Gamlakarleby)

Rovaniemi · Kemijärvi · Sodankylä · Kittilä · Enontekiö

Kuopio · Kajaani · Jyväskylä · KESKI-SUOMEN

Torneträsk · Stora Lulevatten · Uddjaur · Storavan · Storuman · Ångermanälven

Arctic Circle

West from 18° Greenwich

Reykjavik · Keflavík · Hafnarfjörður · Akranes · Akureyri · Húsavík · Siglufjörður · Sauðárkrókur · Seyðisfjörður · Höfn

Vatnajökull · Hofsjökull · Langjökull · Mýrdalsjökull · Eiríksjökull · Snæfellsjökull · Drangajökull

Faxaflói · Breiðafjörður · Arnarfjörður · Ísafjarðardjúp · Húnaflói · Skagafjörður · Eyjafjörður · Héraðsflói

Hekla 1491 · Snæfell 1833 · Hvannadalshnúkur 2119 · Herðubreið 1682 · Askja 1460

Vestmannaeyjar · Surtsey · Ingólfshöfði

NORWEGIAN SEA

RUSSIAN FED.
1. Daghestan Rep.
2. Kabardino–Balkar Rep.
3. Mari Rep.
4. Mordovian Rep.
5. North Ossetian Rep.
6. Tatar Rep.
7. Udmurt Rep.
8. Chuvash Rep.
9. Checheno–Ingush Rep.
AZERBAIJAN
10. Nakhichevan Rep.
GEORGIA
11. Abkhaz Rep.
12. Adzhar Rep.

Projection: Conical Orthomorphic with two standard parallels

East from Greenwich

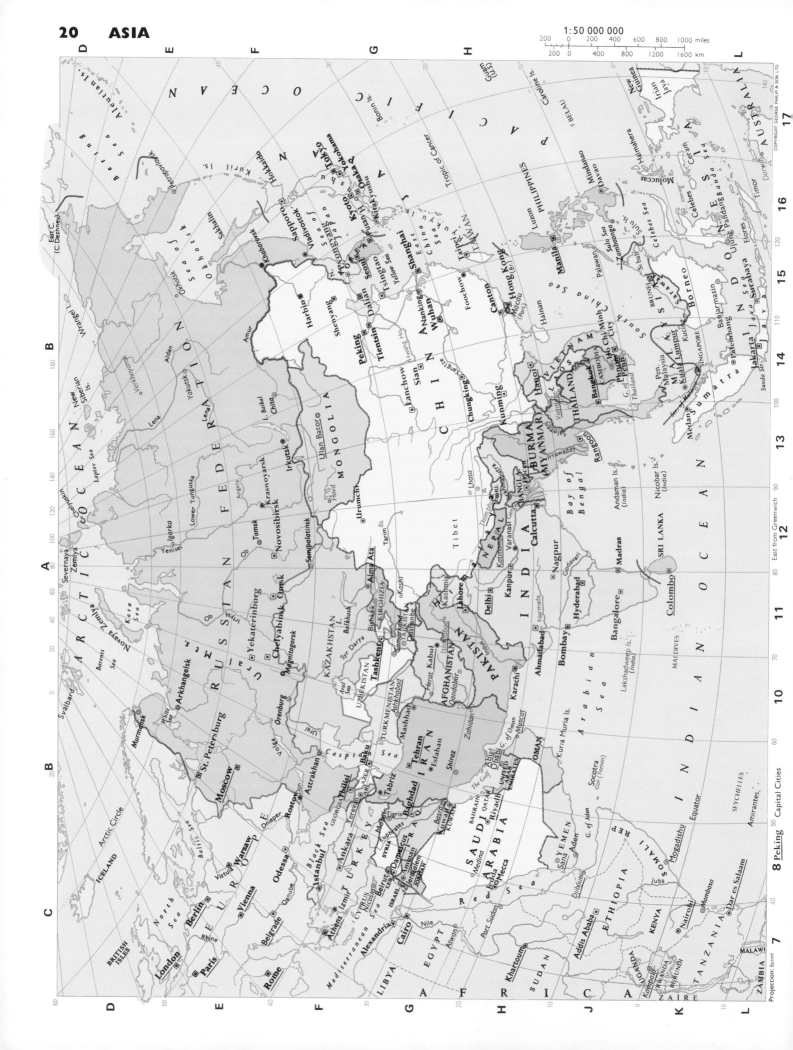

1:20 000 000

100   0   100   200   300   400   500 miles
100   0   200   400   600   800 km

COPYRIGHT GEORGE PHILIP & SON LTD.

CHINA

KIRGHIZIA

UZBEKISTAN

TURKMENISTAN

TAJIKISTAN

Tashkent

Ashkhabad

Aral'skoye More

Plato Ustyurt

Kara Kum

Kizil Kum

AFGHANISTAN

Kabul

Herat

Qandahar

IRAN

Tehrān

Eşfahān

Shīrāz

Kermān

Yazd

Mashhad

Dasht-e Lūt

Dasht-e Kavīr

Zāgros

PAKISTAN

Karachi

Quetta

Indus

INDIA

Bombay

Delhi

Hyderabad

KASHMIR

JAMMU

Srīnagar

Rāwalpindi

Lahore

Multān

Lakshadweep Islands (Laccadive Is.) (India)

ARABIAN SEA

Gulf of Oman

Masqat (Muscat)

OMAN

Socotra (Yemen)

UNITED ARAB EMIRATES

QATAR

BAHRAIN

Al Manāmah

KUWAIT

Al Kuwayt

SAUDI ARABIA

Ar Riyāḍ (Riyadh)

Rub' al Khali

HIJAZ

Makkah

Jiddah

Al Madīnah (Medina)

YEMEN

Şan'ā'

Al 'Adan (Aden)

Gulf of Aden

DJIBOUTI

SOMALI REP.

Berbera

ETHIOPIA

L. Tana

SUDAN

El Khartûm

Omdurman

IRAQ

Baghdād

Al Başrah

Al Mawşil

Karbalā'

Mesopotamia

Tigris

Euphrates

SYRIA

Dimashq (Damascus)

Halab

Hims

LEBANON

Bayrūt

ISRAEL

Tel Aviv

JORDAN

'Ammān

CYPRUS

TURKEY

Ankara

İstanbul

İzmir

Adana

Konya

Black Sea

GEORGIA

Tbilisi

ARMENIA

Yerevan

AZERBAIJAN

Baku

Caspian Sea

Tabrīz

GREECE

Athínai

Mediterranean Sea

Crete

Marmara

EGYPT

El Qâhira (Cairo)

El Iskandarîya (Alexandria)

El Suweis

Nile

Aswân

Asyût

G. of Suez

Red Sea

Tropic of Cancer

East from Greenwich

Projection: Alber's Equal Area with two standard parallels

1:20 000 000

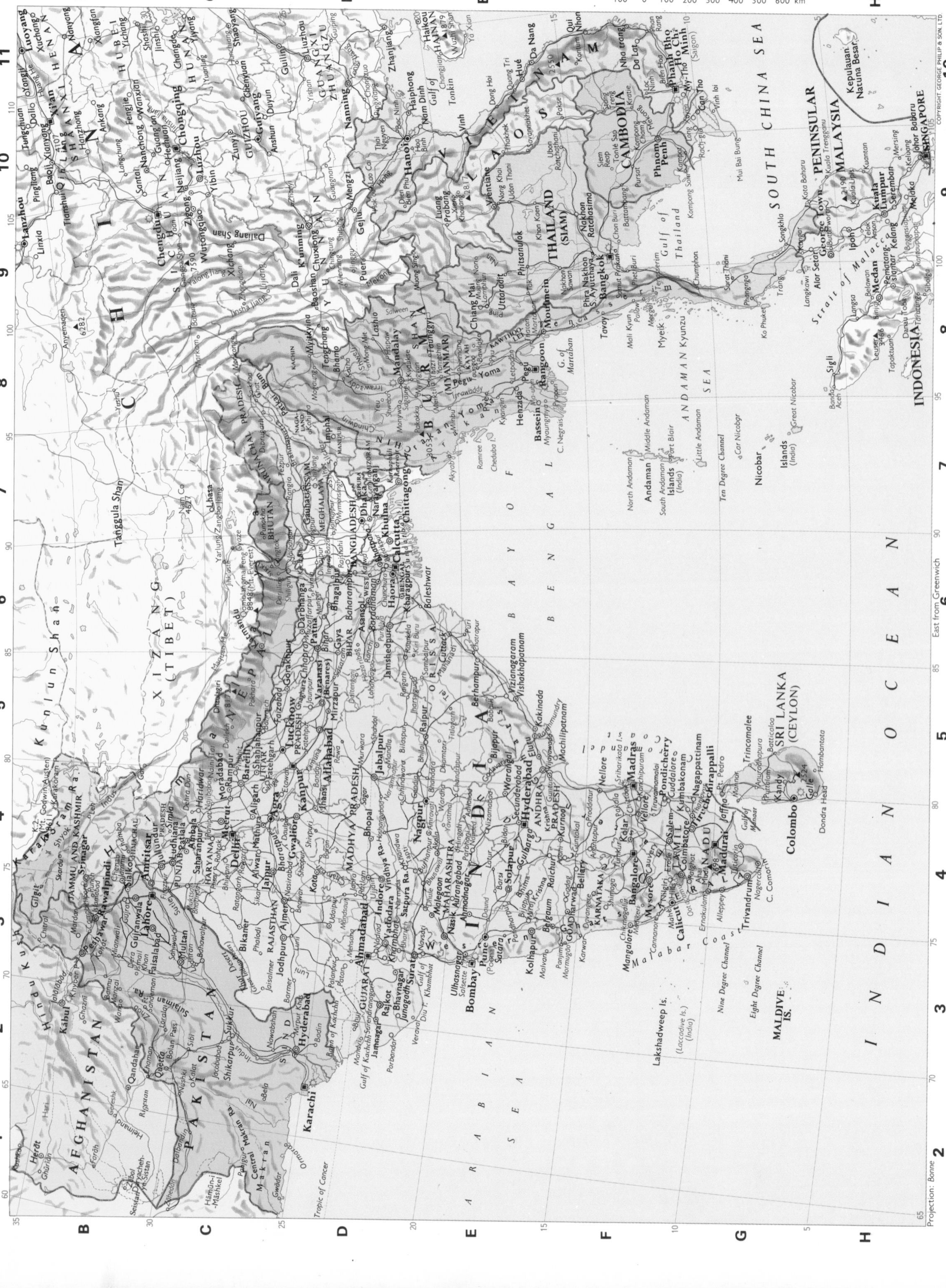
100 0 100 200 300 400 miles
100 0 100 200 300 400 500 600 km
AFGHANISTAN
PAKISTAN
INDIA
XIZANG (TIBET)
CHINA
NEPAL
BHUTAN
BANGLADESH
BURMA (MYANMAR)
THAILAND (SIAM)
LAOS
VIETNAM
CAMBODIA
PENINSULAR MALAYSIA
SINGAPORE
INDONESIA
SRI LANKA (CEYLON)
MALDIVE IS.
ARABIAN SEA
BAY OF BENGAL
ANDAMAN SEA
SOUTH CHINA SEA
INDIAN OCEAN
Gulf of Thailand
Strait of Malacca
Tropic of Cancer
Kunlun Shan
Hindu Kush
Karakoram Ra.
Tanggula Shan
Lakshadweep Is. (Laccadive Is.) (India)
Andaman Islands (India)
Nicobar Islands (India)
Ten Degree Channel
Nine Degree Channel
Eight Degree Channel
Malabar Coast
Karachi
Bombay
Delhi
Calcutta
Madras
Colombo
Rangoon
Bangkok
Hanoi
Kuala Lumpur
Lhasa
Kathmandu
Dhaka
East from Greenwich
Projection: Bonne
COPYRIGHT GEORGE PHILIP & SON, LTD.

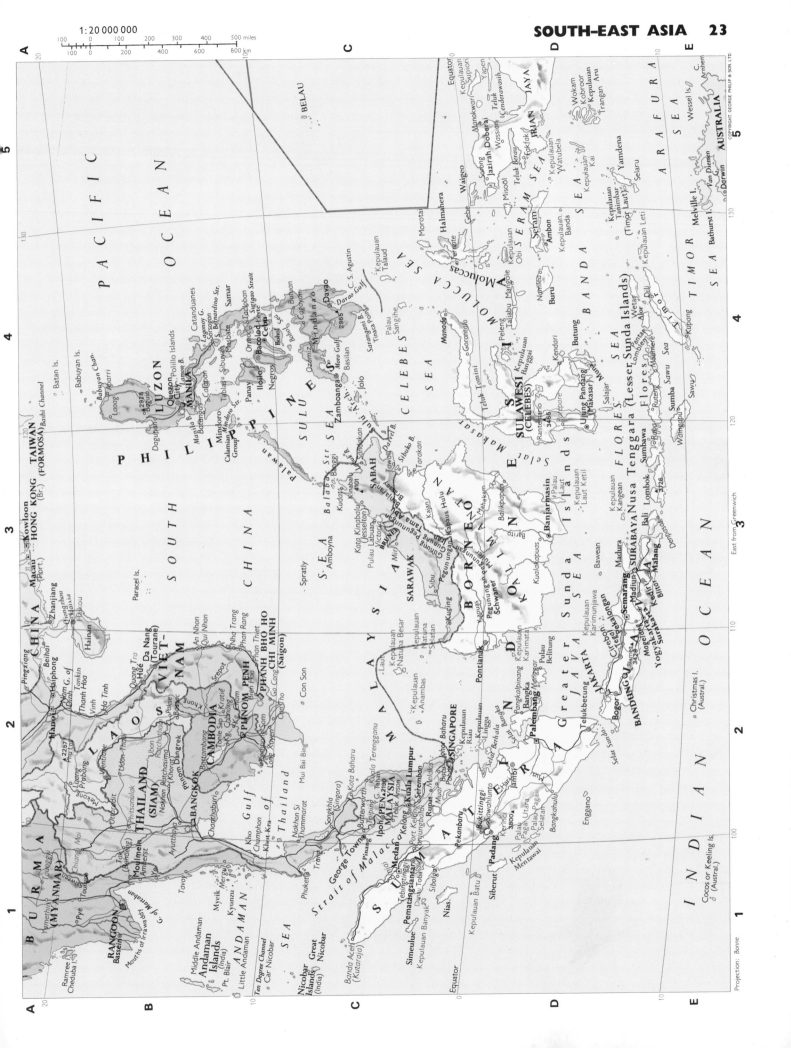

1:20 000 000

Projection: Bonne

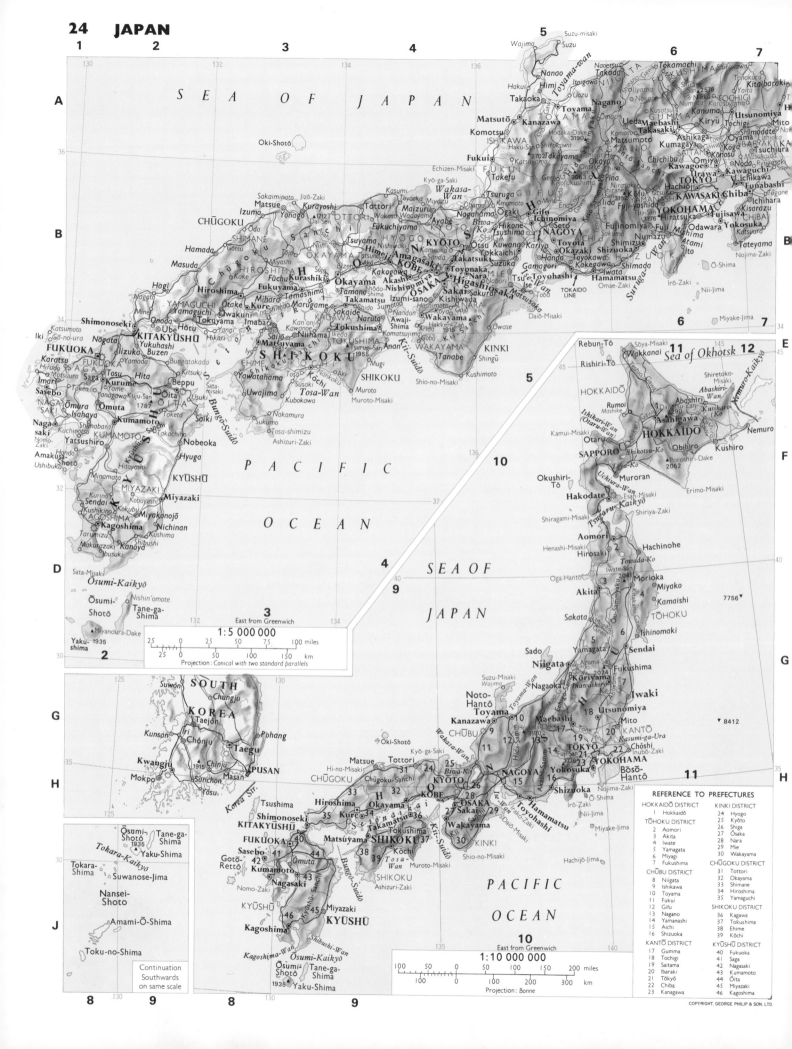

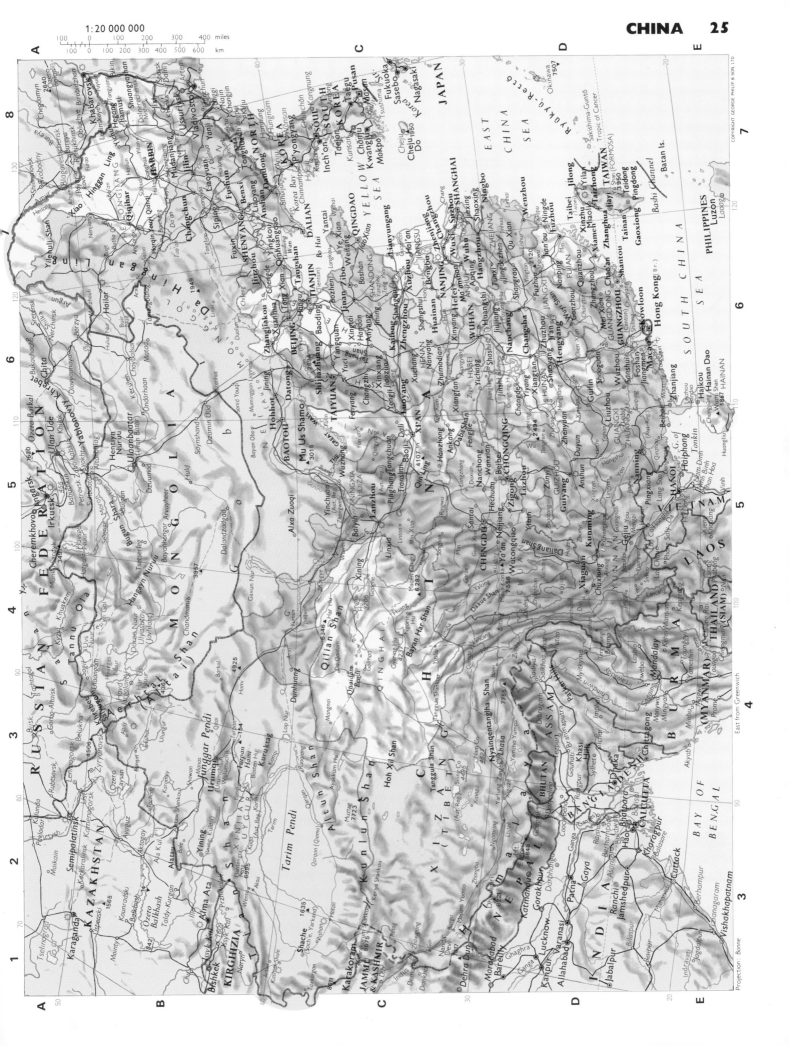

TIMOR SEA

Java Trench

▼6389

Ashmore Reef • Cartier I.

Scott Reef
Koolan & Cockatoo Is.
Rowley Shoals
Lacepede Is.

C. Londonderry
C. Talbot
Vansittart B.
Admiralty G.
Montague Sd.
York Sd.
Brunswick B.
Bonaparte Archipelago
Bougainville
C. Levêque
King Sd.
C. Baskerville
Carnot B.
C. Boileau
C. Latouche Treville
C. Bossut

Jos. Bonaparte Gulf
Cambridge G.
Drysdale
Wyndham
Kununurra
L. Argyle
King Leopold Ras.
Mt. Ord 936
Glenroy
Meda
Derby
Hall's Creek
Fitzroy Crossing
Broome
Roebuck B.
Dampier Downs
La Grange

Mt. Hann 776
Kimberley
Durack Range
DUNCAN
Ord
GREAT NORTHERN
Gordon Downs
Sturt

Croker
Bathurst I.
Melville I.
Dundas Str.
Cobourg Pen.
Goulburn Is.
Junction B.
Crocodile I.
Clarence Str.
P. Darwin
Van' Diemen Gulf
Castlereagh B.
Buckingham
Darwin
Pt. Blaze
Anson B.
Batchelor
Rum Jungle
Frances Creek
Pine Creek
C. Ford
Arnhem Land
Katherine
Roper
Mataranka
Birdum
Larrimah
Victoria
Victoria River Downs
Daly Waters
Wave Hill
Newcastle Waters
L. Woods
Powell Creek
Renner Springs T.O.

Eighty Mile Beach
P. Hedland
Finucane I.
Mount Goldsworthy
Nimingarra
De Grey
Marble Bar
Throssell Ra.
Nullagine
Mt. Nicholas
Robertson Ra.
Newman

Canning Basin
Great Sandy Desert
L. Dora
L. Blanche
L. Disappointment

Gregory Lake
Hordern Hills
The Granites
Mt. Singleton ▲844

NORTHERN TERRITORY
Tanami Desert
Tennant Creek
Barkly
Murchison Ra.
Davenport Ra.
Barrow Creek T.O.
Sando
Mt. Freeling 998
Reynolds Ra.
Mt. Ziel 1510
Mt. Liebig 1524
Mt. Laughlen 1169
Mt. Macdonald
Macdonnell Ras.
James Ra.
Alice Springs
Hugh
Finke
Palmer
Charlot Waters

Dampier Archipelago
Hampton Harb.
Monte Bello Is.
Barrow I.
Dampier
Preston
Roebourne
Pilbara
Deepdale
Onslow
N.W. Cape
Exmouth G.
Exmouth
Learmonth
Pt. Cloates
Mt. Enid
Fortescue
Hamersley Ra.
Wittenoom
Tom Price 1227
Mt. Bruce 1251
Ophthalmia Ra.
Mt. Meharry
Ashburton
Mount Whaleback
Parraburdoo

WESTERN
Gibson Desert
Rawlinson Ra.
L. Macdonald
L. Amadeus
Mt. Olga 1069
Ayers Rock 867
Mt. Woodroffe 1440
Musgrave Ranges
Everard Ras.
Hamilton
Alberga
Oodnadatta
Warrin

C. Farquhar
C. McLeod
C. Cuvier
Geographe Chan.
Bernier I.
Carnarvon
Dorre I.
Naturaliste Chan.
Dirk Hartog
Denham
S. Passage
Steep Pt.
Gascoyne
Wooramel
North West Basin
W. COASTAL
Barlee Ra.
Mt. Augustus 1105
Mt. Egerton 994
Peak Hill
Robinson
Murchison
Sanford
Meekatharra
Nannine
Cue
L. Austin
Sandstone
Tallering Peak 453
Mt. Magnet
Yalgoo

AUSTRALIA
L. Buchanan
L. Carnegie
L. Carey
L. Wells 661
L. Yeo
Wiluna
Laverton
L. Rason
Great Victoria Desert
L. Maurice
Coober Pedy
Stuar

SOUTH AUSTRALIA
Blackstone Ra.
Barrow Ra.

Gantheaume B.
P. Gregory
Houtman Abrolhos
Northampton
Champion B.
Geraldton
Dongara
Mullewa
L. Monger
L. Barlee
L. Moore
Bonnie Rock
Leonora
Malcolm
Menzies
L. Raeside
L. Ballard
Kanowna
Kalgoorlie-Boulder
Coolgardie
Bullfinch
Southern Cross
L. Lefroy
L. Cowan
Norseman
L. Dundas
Zanthus
Premier Downs
Forrest
Rawlinna
Deakin
Eucla Basin
Nullarbor Plain
Hampton Tableland
Eyre
Pt. Dover
Pt. Culver

Maralinga
Ooldea
Tarcoola
L. Harris
L. Everard
Ceduna
L. Gair
Nukey
Peneng
Streaky B.
Nuyts Archipelago
Anxious B.
Eyre Pen.
Coffin B. Penin.
Whidbey Is.
Port Lincoln
C. Catastrophe
Thist
Investigator Group
C. Adieu
Fowlers B.
C. Radstock
Head of Bight

Dampier
Geraldton
Coastal Plains Basin
Jurien B.
Wedge
Dongara
Bencubbin
Northam
Merredin
Kellerberrin
The Johnston Lakes
Beverley
Brookton
Narrogin
Newdegate
Swan
Midland
York
Perth
Fremantle
Kwinana
Pinjarra
Bunbury
Collie
Wagin
Nyabing
Gnowangerup
Doubtful B.
Ravensthorpe
Hopetoun
Esperance
Esperance B.
C. Arid
C. Pasley
Archipelago of the Recherche
C. le Grand
Rocky Pt.

Geographe B.
C. Naturaliste
Busselton
Augusta
C. Leeuwin
Flinders B.
Pt. d'Entrecasteaux
Bridgetown
Manjimup
Pemberton
Katanning
Stirling Ra.
Mt Barker
Pt. Hood
C. Knob
Albany
Denmark
King George Sound
Tor B.
Pt. Nuyts

Great Australian Bight

INDIAN OCEAN

1:6 000 000

NEW ZEALAND & S.W. PACIFIC
1:60 000 000

SAMOA ISLANDS
1:12 000 000

WESTERN SAMOA — AMERICAN SAMOA

Savai'i Apia Upolu Pago Pago Manua Is. Tutuila Rose I.

Wallis & Futuna (Fr.) WESTERN SAMOA

FIJI AND TONGA ISLANDS
1:12 000 000

FIJI — Vanua Levu — Taveuni — Viti Levu — Suva — Kandavu

TONGA (Friendly Is.) — Niuafo'ou — Vava'u — Tofua I. — Tongatapu — Nuku'alofa

Inset: New Zealand & S.W. Pacific
KIRIBATI — TUVALU (Ellice Is.) — Tokelau Is. (N.Z.) — Tongareva (Penrhyn) I. — Pukapuka — Rakahanga — Manihiki — Nassau — Suwarrow — Northern Group — WESTERN SAMOA — Savai'i — Upolu — Tutuila — AMER. SAMOA (U.S.) — Cook Is. (N.Z.) — Palmerston — Atoll — Aitutaki — Mitiaro — Mauke — Rarotonga — Mangaia — Îles de la Société — Niue (N.Z.) — TONGA (Friendly Is.) — Lower Group — FRENCH POLYNESIA — Wallis & Futuna (Fr.) — Rotuma — Lau or Eastern Group — FIJI — Vanua Levu — Viti Levu — VANUATU — Tropic of Capricorn — PACIFIC OCEAN — Macauley — Raoul (Sunday) I. — Kermadec Is. (N.Z.) — Curtis — Three Kings Is. — Auckland — NORTH I. — Cook Strait — NEW ZEALAND — Wellington — Chatham I. — Chatham Is. — Pitt I. — SOUTH I. — Christchurch — Tasman Sea — Dunedin — Bounty Is. — Stewart I. — Snares — Antipodes Is. — Campbell I. — Auckland Is. — Macquarie (Austr.) — SOUTHERN OCEAN

North Island
NORTH ISLAND — Three Kings Is. — C. Reinga — C. Maria van Diemen — North C. — Houhora — Rangaunu Bay — Doubtless Bay — Whangaroa Bay — Ahipara B. — Kaitaia — Tauroa Pt. — Bay of Islands — C. Brett — Rawene — Hokianga Harb. — Kaikohe — Hikurangi — Donnelly's Crossing — Whangarei — Whangarei Harb. — Bream Hd. — Dargaville — Waipu — Bream Bay — Lit. Barrier I. — Gt. Barrier I. — C. Rodney — Kaipara Harb. — Warkworth — Cuvier I. — Helensville — Hauraki Gulf — Coromandel — Takapuna — Devonport — AUCKLAND — Whitianga — Onehunga — Manukau — Papakura — Thames — Mayor I. — Waiuku — Pukekohe — Tauranga Harb. — Mercer — Waihi — White I. — C. Runaway — Waikato — Paeroa — Mt. Maunganui — East C. — Huntly — Morrinsville — Tauranga — Te Puke — Bay of Plenty — Raglan — Hamilton — Cambridge — Whakatane — Opotiki — Raukumara Ra. — Hikurangi — Kawhia Harb. — Te Awamutu — Putaruru — Rotorua — Tarawera — Kaeo — Waipiro — Mokau — Te Kuiti — Mangakino — Kinleith — Murupara — Tolaga Bay — North Taranaki Bight — Taumarunui — L. Taupo — Taupo — Kaingaroa Forest — Ormond — Gisborne — Waitara — Ongarue — Turangi — Poverty Bay — New Plymouth — Inglewood — Whangamomona — Kaimanawa Mts. — Wairoa — Waikokopu — Mt. Egmont — Stratford — Ruapehu — Taihape — Ruahine Ra. — Mahia Peninsula — Opunake — Eltham — Kopua — Ohakune — Waiouru — Bay Hawke Bay — Hawera — Waverley — Taihape — Napier — South Taranaki Bight — Mangaweka — C. Kidnappers — Wanganui — Hunterville — Hastings — Marton — Halcombe — Waipawa — Bulls — Feilding — Waipukurau — Palmerston N. — Dannevirke — Foxton — Shannon — Woodville — Pahiatua — C. Turnagain — Levin — Otaki — Eketahuna — Paraparaumu — Kapiti I. — Feathertston — Masterton — Carterton — Greytown — Up. Hutt — Petone — Lr. Hutt — Martinborough — WELLINGTON — Cook Strait

South Island
SOUTH ISLAND — C. Farewell — Collingwood — Golden Bay — Takaka — D'Urville I. — Tasman Mts. — Tasman Bay — Motueka — Pelorus Sd. — Karamea Bight — Nelson — Richmond — Picton — Karamea — Wakefield — Havelock — Blenheim — Seddonville — Wairau — Seddon — Granity — Lyell Ra. — Ward — Westport — Lyell — Murchison — Tadmor — Inangahua Junction — Rotoroa — Mt. Travers 2338 — Marlborough — Reefton — Grey — Spenser Mts. — Kaikoura — Blackball — Runanga — Hanmer — Amuri P. — Springs — Clarence — Greymouth — Kumara — Stillwater — Waiau — Kaikoura — Hokitika — L. Brunner — Jacksons — Poura — Culverden — Waiau — Ross — Arthur's Pass — Waikari — Hurunui — Abut Hd. — Okarito — Waipara — Oxford — Pegasus Bay — Coleridge — Rangiora — Kaiapoi — New Brighton — Whitecliffs — Springfield — Christchurch — Mt. Cook 3753 — Lincoln — Lyttelton — Methven — Riccarton — Akaroa — Mt. Cook — L. Tekapo — Staveley — Rakaia — Banks Peninsula — L. Ellesmere — Little River — Jackson B. — Okuru — Fairlie — Southern Alps — Rotherham — Ashburton Bight — Temuka — Timaru — W. Mt. Aspiring 3027 — L. Ohau — Pukaki — St. Andrews — Wanaka — Canterbury Bight — Milford Sd. — Mt. Earnslaw 2819 — L. Wanaka — Waimate — Bligh Sd. — Kurow — Waimate — George Sd. — Arrowtown — Cromwell — Tokarahi — Ngapara — Queenstown — Clyde — Kakanui Mts. — Oamaru — Secretary I. — Wakatipu — Alexandra — Naseby — Maheno — Doubtful Sd. — Garvie Mts. — Roxburgh — Hampden — Dunback — Palmerston — Manapouri — Umbrella Mts. — Waikouaiti — Breaksea Sd. — Te Anau — Kingston — Otago — Edievale — Lawrence — Port Chalmers — Resolution I. — Lumsden — Mossburn — Fairfield — Otago Harbour — Dusky Sd. — Mosgiel — Dunedin — St. Kilda — C. Saunders — L. Te Anau — Southland — Ohai — Clinton — Milton — Chalky Inlet — Tuatapere — Nightcaps — Balclutha — Preservation Inlet — Winton — Gore — Mataura — Kaitangata — Nugget Pt. — Te Waewae B. — Orepuki — Wyndham — Owaka — Riverton — Invercargill — Otautau — Foveaux Str. — Bluff — Ruapuke I. — Stewart I. — Halfmoon Bay — Port Pegasus — S.W. Cape

TASMAN SEA — PACIFIC OCEAN

Projection: Conical with two standard parallels

COPYRIGHT. GEORGE PHILIP & SON. LTD.

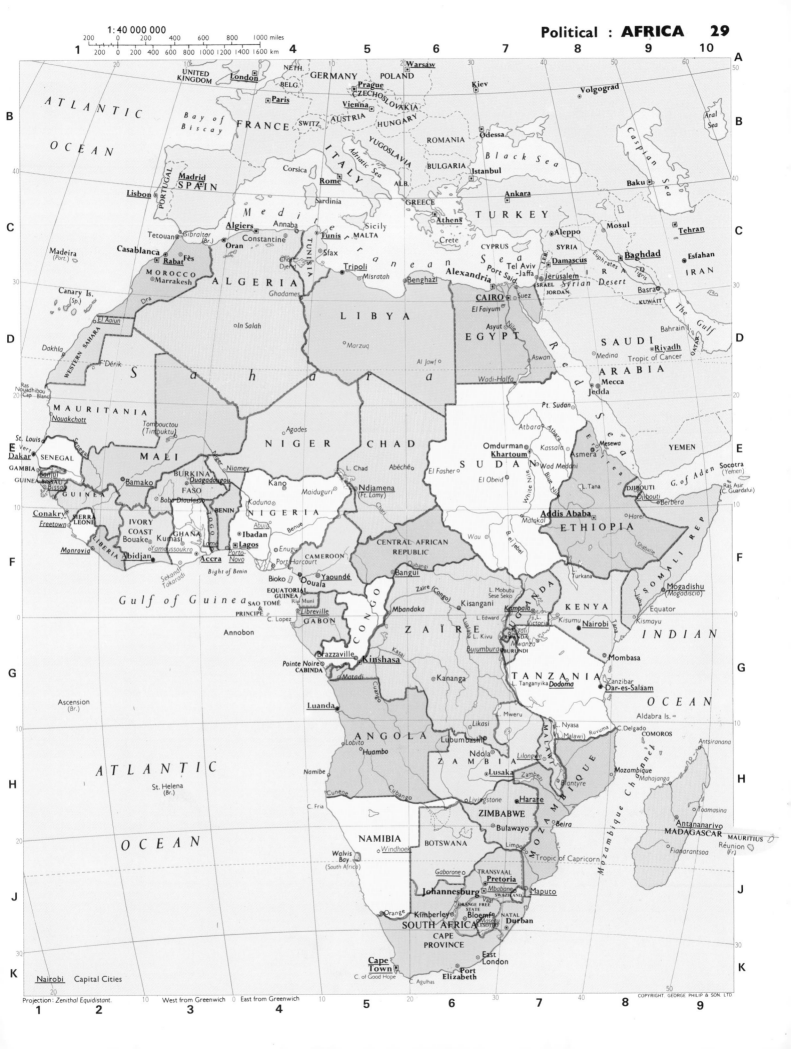

NORTH ATLANTIC OCEAN

SPAIN

Cádiz · Málaga · Almería
Cabo de São Vicente
Str. of Gibraltar · Gibraltar (Br.)
Tanger · Ceuta (Sp.) · Sidi-Bel-Abbès · Oran · Mostaganem · Ech Cheliff · Alger (Algiers) · El Harrach · Tizi-Ouzou · Bejaïa · Skikda · Annaba
Tétouan · Melilla · Blida · Medéa · Constantine · Guelma · Sétif · Batna
Larache · Ksar el Kebir · Oujda · Tlemcen · Saïda · El Aricha · Djelfa · Biskra · Khenchela
Kenitra (Port Lyautey) · Salé · Fès · Taza · Jerada
Rabat · Meknès
Casablanca · Berrechid · Khenifra · Bou Arfa · Laghouat · El Oued
El Jadida · Settat · Khouribga · 2235 · Ghardaïa · Touggourt
Safi · Essaouira · Marrakech · Beni Mellal · Ar Rachidya · Béchar · El Goléa · Hassi Messaoud · Ft. Lallemand
Ras Beddouza
C. Rhir · Toubkal 4165 · Ouarzazate · Abadla · Beni Abbès · Ft. Lallemand · Hassi el Gassi
Agadir · Taroudannt · Igli · Kerzaz · Ghudâmis
Anti Atlas · Ifni · Tiznit · Dra · Mengoub · Timimoun · Hassi Inifel · Ohanet

MOROCCO · Haut Atlas · Moyen Atlas · Atlas Saharien
Haut Atlas · 2308

ALGERIA
Plateau du Tademaït
Adrar · In Belbel · In Salah · Bordj Omar Driss
Bj. Fly Ste. Marie · Miliana · Aoulef el Arab · Illizi
Zaouiet Reggane · Arak · Bj.-in-Eker · Idelès · Djanet

Islas Canarias (Sp.)
Lanzarote
La Palma · Fuerteventura · Arrecife
Tenerife · Sta. Cruz · Puerto del Rosario
Gomera · Gran Canaria · Las Palmas
Hierro
C. Juby · Tarfaya (Villa Bens)
El Aaiún
Semara
Bu Craa
C. Bojador · Aïn Ben Tili · Chegga
Bir Mogrein

Madeira (Port.) · Pto. Santo · Funchal
6578

WESTERN SAHARA
Dakhla · Pta. Durnford
C. Barbas · Fderik · Zouérate · Terhazza
Nouâdhibou (Port Etienne) · Chär · Taoudenni · Tanezrouft · Ahaggar · Tahat 2918
Ras La Güera · Nouâdhibou · Poste Maurice-Cortier (Bidon 5) · Tamanrasset
Atâr · Ouadâne · Adrar des Iforhas · Admer
Oujeft · Chinguetti · Tessalit

MAURITANIA · El Djouf
Akjoujt · Mabrouk · Aïr (Azbine) · Monts Tamgak
Nouakchott · Rachid · Tidjikja · Tichît · Araouane · Kidal · Iférouâne 1900
Boutilimit · Moudjéria · Akreïjit · Bou Djébéha · Agadez
Aleg · Tagba · Oualâta · I-n-Gall
Mederdra · Tâmchekket · Tombouctou · Bamba · Bourem · Kerchoual
St. Louis · Bogué · Kiffa · Néma · Goundam · Diré · Kabara · Gourma-Rharous · Gaő · Ménaka

NIGER

Dagana · Matam · Sélibabi · Nioro du Sahel · Niafounké · Hombori · Ansongo
Louga · Linguère · Nara · Tahoua · Tamaské · Gangara
Tivaouane · Dahra · Yélimané · Sokolo · Douentza · Famalé · Filingué · Birni Nkonni · Zinder
Rufisque · Thiès · Diourbel · Tiel · Bakel · Mourdiah · Mopti · Djibo · Dori · Téra · Tillabéri · Madaoua · Kelgi
Dakar · Kaolack · Kayes · Ké-Macina · Ségou · Bandiagara · Niamey · Say · Dosso

SENEGAL · Didièni · Sokolo · Douentza
GAMBIA · Tambacounda · Kita · Banamba · Koutiala · **BURKINA** · Dogondoutchi · Birnin-Kebbi · Maradi · Katsina
Banjul · Maka · Bafoulabé · Douna · **FASO** · Fada N'Gourma · Gaya · Jega · Gummi · Kano
Sedhiou · Georgetown · Kolda · Satadougou · Séguin · Sikasso · Bobo-Dioulasso · Ouagadougou · Hadejia
GUINEA-BISSAU · Kédougou · Kankan · Bougouni · Léo · Tenkodogo · Kende · Shanga · Zaria
Ziguinchor · Fouta Djalon · Touqué · Dinguiraye · Banfora · Diébougou · Pô · Kaïama · Kaduna
Bissau · Bafatá · Dabola · Kissidougou · Tingréla · Tumu · Gambaga · Nikki · Minna · Jos

GUINEA · Conakry · Forécariah · Faranah · Odienné · IVORY COAST · Koro · Bouna · Wa · Tamale · Parakou · Abuja
Freetown · **SIERRA LEONE** · Makeni · Beyla · Mankono · Katiola · Bondoukou · Kintampo · **TOGO** · **BENIN** · Ilorin · Offa · Oshogbo · Ife
LIBERIA · Man · Danané · Daloa · Bouaké · Séguéla · Wenchi · Kumasi · Abomey · Oyo · Ibadan · Benin City
Monrovia · Yamoussoukro · Dimbokro · Obuasi · **GHANA** · Kpalimé · Lomé · Porto-Novo · Lagos · Onitsha
NIGERIA
Buchanan · Tabou · Abidjan · Sekondi-Takoradi · Accra · Tema · Cotonou · Aba · Port-Harcourt · **CAMEROON**
Bight of Benin · Bioko · Malabo · Douala

NIGER
CHAD
NIGERIA
CAMEROON
CENTRAL AFRICAN REPUBLIC
SUDAN
ETHIOPIA
KENYA
UGANDA
TANZANIA
ZAÏRE
CONGO
GABON
EQUATORIAL GUINEA
RWANDA
BURUNDI
CABINDA
Khartoum
El Khartûm
Omdurmân
Asmera
Addis Abeba
Nairobi
Mombasa
Dar-es-Salaam
Zanzibar
Kampala
Kigali
Bujumbura
Kisangani
Kinshasa
Brazzaville
Luanda
Libreville
Douala
Yaoundé
Ndjamena
Bangui
Kano
Maiduguri
Pointe Noire
Mbandaka
Kananga
Mbuji-Mayi
El Obeid
Wad Medani
L. Victoria
L. Tana
Lac Tchad
L. Turkana (L. Rudolf)
L. Tanganyika
Zaïre
Ubangi
Kasai
Lualaba

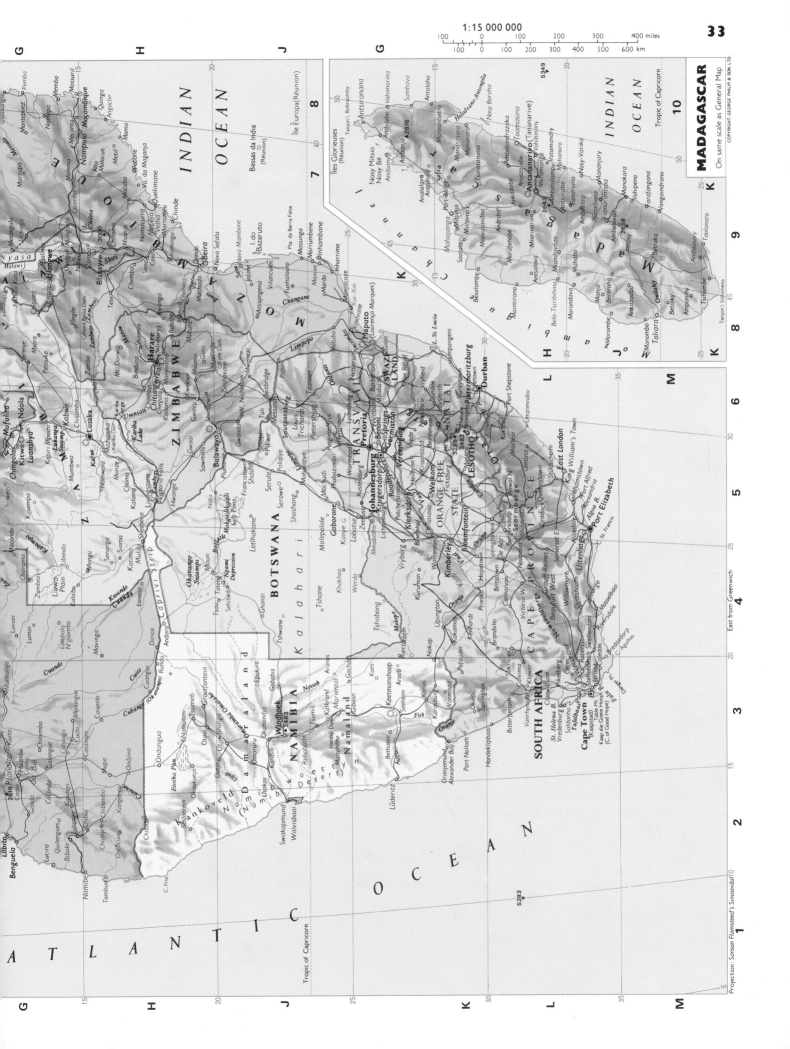

1:15 000 000

100   0   100   200   300   400 miles
100   0   100   200   300   400   500   600 km

MADAGASCAR
On same scale as General Map

COPYRIGHT GEORGE PHILIP & SON, LTD.

INDIAN OCEAN

ATLANTIC OCEAN

Tropic of Capricorn

East from Greenwich

Projection : Sanson Flamsteed's Sinusoidal

Projection: Bonne

ALASKA
1:30 000 000

100　0　100　200　300 miles

100　0　200　400　km

West from Greenwich

HAWAII
1:10 000 000

Projection: Albers' Equal Area with two standard parallels

West from Greenwich

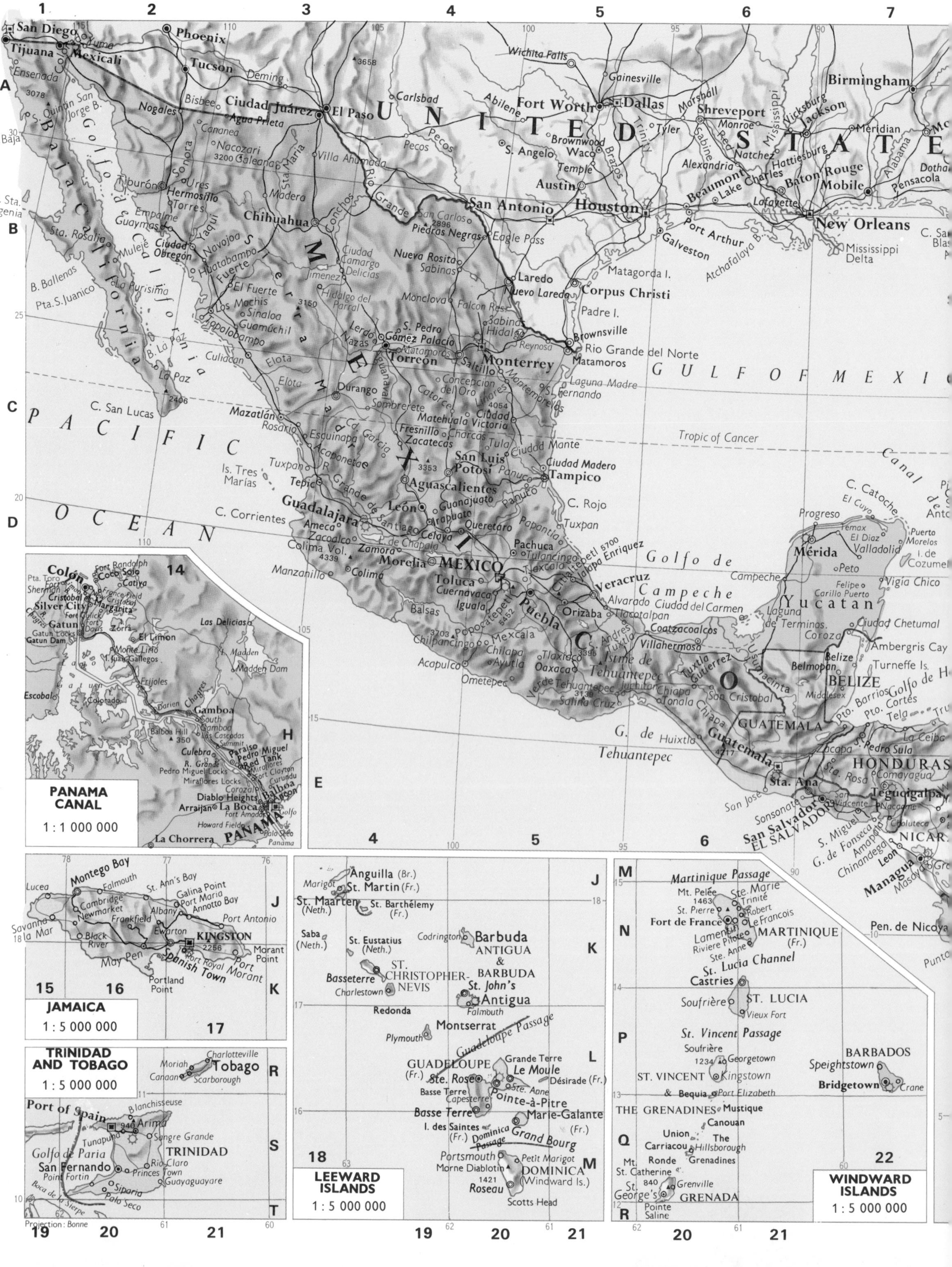

UNITED STATES
MEXICO
GULF OF MEXICO
PACIFIC OCEAN
Golfo de Campeche
Yucatan
Tropic of Cancer
Baja California
Golfo de California
Sierra Madre
San Diego
Tijuana
Mexicali
Yuma
Ensenada
Phoenix
Tucson
Deming
Bisbee
Nogales
Ciudad Juárez
El Paso
Agua Prieta
Cananea
Nacozari
Galeana
Villa Ahumada
Carlsbad
Pecos
Wichita Falls
Gainesville
Abilene
Fort Worth
Dallas
Tyler
Marshall
Shreveport
Monroe
Vicksburg
Jackson
Birmingham
Meridian
Brownwood
Waco
S. Angelo
Temple
Austin
Natchez
Alexandria
Hattiesburg
Baton Rouge
Mobile
Pensacola
Beaumont
Lake Charles
Lafayette
New Orleans
San Antonio
Houston
Port Arthur
Galveston
Mississippi Delta
Eagle Pass
Piedras Negras
San Carlos
Laredo
Nuevo Laredo
Corpus Christi
Matagorda I.
Padre I.
Brownsville
Matamoros
Rio Grande del Norte
Reynosa
Laguna Madre
Hermosillo
Tiburón
Ures
Torres
Empalme
Guaymas
Ciudad Obregón
Navojoa
Huatabampo
Fuerte
El Fuerte
Los Mochis
Sinaloa
Guamúchil
Topolobampo
Culiacán
Chihuahua
Madera
Ciudad Camargo
Delicias
Jimenez
Hidalgo del Parral
Sta. Rosalia
Mulejé
B. Ballenas
Pta. S. Juanico
La Purísima
B. La Paz
La Paz
C. San Lucas
Pta. Baja
Pta. Sta. Eugenia
S. Quintín
San Jorge B.
Nueva Rosita
Sabinas
Monclova
Falcon Res.
Sabinas Hidalgo
Monterrey
Saltillo
Gómez Palacio
Torreón
Lerdo
Nazas
S. Pedro
Matamoros
Durango
Concepcion del Oro
Linares
Montemorelos
S. Fernando
Catorce
Matehuala
Ciudad Victoria
Sombrerete
Fresnillo
Charcas
Zacatecas
Tula
Ciudad Mante
San Luis Potosí
Ciudad Madero
Tampico
Mazatlán
Rosario
Escuinapa
Acaponeta
Tuxpan
Tepic
Is. Tres Marías
Aguascalientes
León
Guanajuato
Irapuato
Celaya
Querétaro
Guadalajara
Ameca
Zacoalco
L. de Chapala
Zamora
Morelia
Colima Vol.
Colima
Manzanillo
C. Corrientes
C. Rojo
Tuxpan
Papantla
Pachuca
Tulancingo
MEXICO
Toluca
Cuernavaca
Iguala
Tlaxcala
Puebla
Popocatepetl
Citlaltepetl
Jalapa Enriquez
Veracruz
Orizaba
Alvarado
Tlacotalpan
Balsas
Chilpancingo
Chilapa
Mexcala
Acapulco
Ayutla
Ometepec
Tlaxiaco
Oaxaca
Coatzacoalcos
Villahermosa
Ciudad del Carmen
Laguna de Terminos
Campeche
Istmo de Tehuantepec
Tehuantepec
Juchitán
Salina Cruz
G. de Tehuantepec
Tuxtla Gutiérrez
Chiapa
Tonala
San Cristobal
Huixtla
Progreso
Mérida
Valladolid
Peto
Felipe Carillo Puerto
Vigía Chico
Puerto Morelos
I. de Cozumel
C. Catoche
Canal de Yucatan
Ciudad Chetumal
Corozal
Ambergris Cay
Belize
Belmopan
Turneffe Is.
BELIZE
Middlesex
Golfo de Honduras
Pto. Barrios
Pto. Cortés
Tela
La Ceiba
GUATEMALA
Guatemala
Zacapa
S. Pedro Sula
HONDURAS
Comayagua
Tegucigalpa
Sta. Ana
Sonsonate
San Salvador
EL SALVADOR
S. Miguel
G. de Fonseca
Choluteca
Chinandega
Leon
Managua
Masaya
NICARAGUA
Pen. de Nicoya
San José

PANAMA CANAL
1 : 1 000 000
Colón
Fort Randolph
Coco Solo
Catiya
Cristobal
Fort Gulick
Silver City
Margarita
Gatun
Gatun Locks
Gatun Dam
Fort Davis
Las Delicias
El Limon
Madden
Madden Dam
Frijoles
Escobal
Colorado
Darien
Chagres
Gamboa
Balboa Hill
Culebra
Paraiso
Pedro Miguel
Red Tank
Pedro Miguel Locks
Miraflores Locks
Corozal
Diablo Heights
Balboa
Ancon
Arraiján
La Boca
Fort Amador
Howard Field
La Chorrera
PANAMA

JAMAICA
1 : 5 000 000
Montego Bay
Lucea
Falmouth
St. Ann's Bay
Galina Point
Port Maria
Annotto Bay
Savanna la Mar
Cambridge
Newmarket
Frankfield
Albany
Ewarton
Port Antonio
Black River
May Pen
Spanish Town
KINGSTON
Port Royal
Port Morant
Morant Point
Portland Point

TRINIDAD AND TOBAGO
1 : 5 000 000
Tobago
Charlotteville
Moriah
Canaan
Scarborough
Port of Spain
Blanchisseuse
Arima
Sangre Grande
Tunapuna
TRINIDAD
Golfo de Paria
San Fernando
Point Fortin
Rio Claro
Princes Town
Guayaguayare
Siparia
Palo Seco
Boca de la Sierpe

LEEWARD ISLANDS
1 : 5 000 000
Anguilla (Br.)
Marigot
St. Martin (Fr.)
St. Maarten (Neth.)
St. Barthélemy (Fr.)
Saba (Neth.)
St. Eustatius (Neth.)
Codrington
Barbuda
ANTIGUA & BARBUDA
Basseterre
ST. CHRISTOPHER-NEVIS
Charlestown
St. John's
Antigua
Falmouth
Redonda
Montserrat
Plymouth
Guadeloupe Passage
GUADELOUPE (Fr.)
Grande Terre
Le Moule
Ste. Rose
Désirade (Fr.)
Basse Terre
Capesterre
Ste. Anne
Pointe-à-Pitre
Marie-Galante (Fr.)
I. des Saintes (Fr.)
Grand Bourg
Dominica Passage
Portsmouth
Petit Marigot
Morne Diablotin
DOMINICA (Windward Is.)
Roseau
Scotts Head

WINDWARD ISLANDS
1 : 5 000 000
Martinique Passage
Mt. Pelée
Ste. Marie
St. Pierre
Trinité
Robert
Fort de France
Le Francois
Lamentin
MARTINIQUE (Fr.)
Riviere Pilote
Ste. Anne
St. Lucia Channel
Castries
Soufrière
ST. LUCIA
Vieux Fort
St. Vincent Passage
Soufrière
Georgetown
ST. VINCENT
Kingstown
Bequia
Port Elizabeth
THE GRENADINES
Mustique
Canouan
Union
Carriacou
Hillsborough
The Grenadines
Mt. St. Catherine
Ronde
Grenville
St. George's
GRENADA
Pointe Saline
BARBADOS
Speightstown
Bridgetown
Crane

Projection: Bonne

39

1:15 000 000

NICARAGUA
COSTA RICA
PANAMA
Islas del Maíz (Nic., U.S.)
I. de San Andrés (Colombia)
Cayos de Albuquerque (Colombia)

Barranquilla
Santa Marta
Cartagena
Maracaibo
VENEZUELA
CARACAS
Port of Spain
TRINIDAD & TOBAGO
GRENADA
Curaçao (Neth.)
Aruba (Neth.)

Medellín
Bucaramanga
Cúcuta
San Cristóbal
COLOMBIA
BOGOTÁ
Cali
Armenia
Pereira
Manizales
Buenaventura
Tunja

GUYANA
Mt. Roraima 2810
Sierra Pacaraima
RORAIMA

Tumaco
Pasto
ECUADOR
Quito
Guayaquil
Cuenca
Riobamba
Manta
Chimborazo 6267
Cotopaxi 5896

Negro
Solimões
AMAZONAS
Amazonas
Iquitos
Manaus

Talara
Sullana
Piura
Chiclayo
Trujillo
Chimbote
PERU
LIMA
Callao
Huancayo
Ayacucho
Cuzco
Arequipa
Mollendo

Huascarán 6768

ACRE
Rio Branco
RONDÔNIA
Porto Velho
Guajará-Mirim

BOLIVIA
La Paz
Cochabamba
Santa Cruz
Oruro
Sucre
Potosí
Lago Titicaca
Illimani 6462

Iquique
Tocopilla
Tarija

ARGENTINA
PARAGUAY
Chaco Boreal

PACIFIC OCEAN
Equator
Malpelo (Colombia)
Milne Edwards Trench
Peru Trench
Chile Trench

Projection: Sanson-Flamsteed's Sinusoidal

1:16 000 000

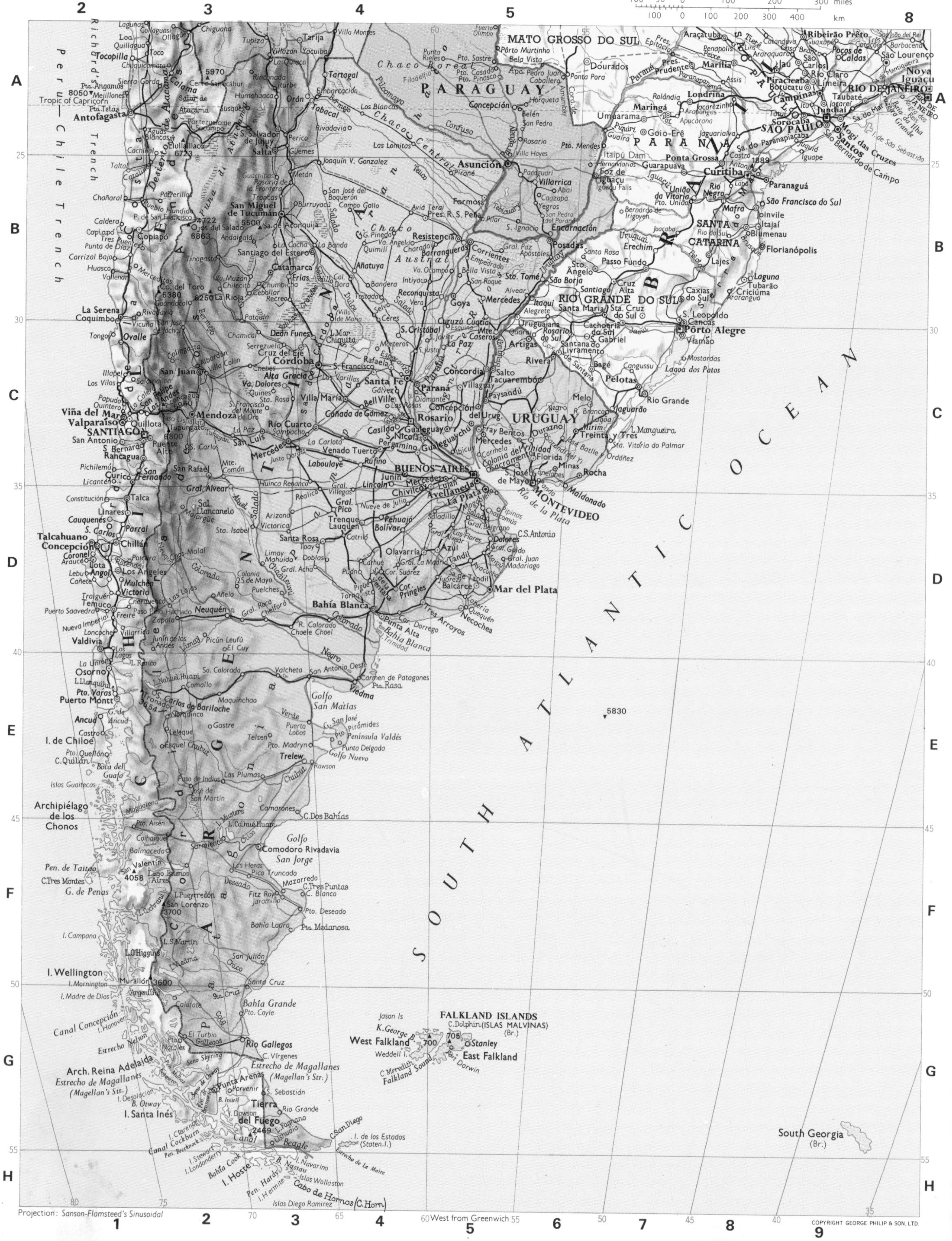

100 50 0 100 200 300 miles
100 0 100 200 300 400 km

PARAGUAY

MATO GROSSO DO SUL

PARANÁ

B R A Z I L

RIO GRANDE DO SUL

SANTA CATARINA

URUGUAY

A R G E N T I N A

C H I L E

SOUTH ATLANTIC OCEAN

Tropic of Capricorn

Peru—Chile Trench

Antofagasta

SANTIAGO

Valparaíso
Viña del Mar

Mendoza

Córdoba

Rosario

BUENOS AIRES

La Plata

MONTEVIDEO

RIO DE JANEIRO

SÃO PAULO

Santos

Curitiba

Pôrto Alegre

Bahía Blanca

Mar del Plata

Neuquén

Valdivia

Puerto Montt

Comodoro Rivadavia
San Jorge

Golfo San Jorge

Río Gallegos

Punta Arenas

Tierra del Fuego

Estrecho de Magallanes
(Magellan's Str.)

Cabo de Hornos (C. Horn)

FALKLAND ISLANDS
(ISLAS MALVINAS)
(Br.)
West Falkland   East Falkland
Stanley

South Georgia
(Br.)

Projection: Sanson-Flamsteed's Sinusoidal

West from Greenwich

INDEX

The index contains the names of all the principal places and features shown on the maps. Each name is followed by an additional entry in italics giving the country or region within which it is located.

Physical features composed of a proper name (Erie) and a description (Lake) are positioned alphabetically by the proper name. The description is positioned after the proper name and is usually abbreviated.

The number in bold type which follows each name in the index refers to the number of the map page where that feature or place will be found. This is usually the largest scale at which the place or feature appears. the letter and figure which are in bold type immediately after the page number give the grid square on the map page, within which the feature is situated. The letter represents the latitude and figure the longitude.

In some cases the feature itself may fall within the specified square, while the name is outside. This is usually the case only with features which are larger than a grid square. Rivers are indexed to their mouths or confluences, and carry the symbol ≈ after their names. A solid ■ follows the name of a country while, an open □ refers to a first order administrative area.

Abbreviations used in the index:

Afghan. - Afghanistan	Dom. Rep. - Dominican Republic	N. - North	Str. - Strait
Arch. - Archipelago	Eq. - Equatorial	N.Z. - New Zealand	Swed. - Sweden
Amer. - America	Fin. - Finland	Neth. - Netherlands	Switz. - Switzerland
Atl. - Atlantic	G. - Gulf	Norw. - Norway	U.A.E. - United Arab Emirates
B. - Bay	Ger. - Germany	Pac. - Pakistan	U.K. - United Kingdom
Bulg. - Bulgaria	I(s). - Island(s), Isle(s)	Pen. - Peninsula	U.S.A. - United States of America
C. - Cape	Ind. - Indian	Port. - Portugal	W. - West
Cent. - Central	Ire. - Ireland	Rep. - Republic	Yug. - Yugoslavia
Chan. - Channel	L. - Lake, Loch, Lough	Rom. - Romania	
Czech. - Czechoslovakia	Mong. - Mongolia	S. - South	
Den. - Denmark	Mt(s). - Mount(s), Mountains(s)	S. Arabia - Saudi Arabia	

A

achen, Ger. 10 C3
pa, Nigeria 30 G6
padan, Iran 21 B3
bashiri, Japan 24 F11
obeville, France 12 A4
beokuta, Nigeria 30 G5
berdare, U.K. 7 F4
berdeen, U.K. 8 D6
berystwyth, U.K. 7 E3
bidjan, Ivory Coast 30 G4
chill I., Ire. 9 C1
concagua, Argentina 42 C3
cre, Brazil 40 E4
damaoua, Massif de l', Cameroon 32 C2
dana, Turkey 21 B2
ddis Abeba, Ethiopia 32 G4
delaide, Australia 27 E6
den, Gulf of, Asia 21 D3
driatic Sea, Italy 14 C6
Egean Sea, Greece 15 E11
fghanistan, ■ Asia 21 C4
frica 29
gadir, Morocco 30 B3
gra, India 22 C4
guascalientes, Mexico 38 C4
haggar, Algeria 30 D6
hmadabad, India 22 D3
hvāz, Iran 21 B3
irdrie, U.K. 8 F5
jaccio, France 14 D3
kershus, Norw. 17 F11
kita, Japan 24 G11
kron, U.S.A. 37 B10
kureyri, Iceland 16 D4
l 'Adan, Yemen 21 D3
l Basrah, Iraq 21 B3
l Hillah, Iraq 21 B3
l Hufūf, S. Arabia 21 C3
l Kut, Iraq 21 B3
l Kuwayt, Kuwait 21 C3
l Madinah, S. Arabia 21 C2
l Manamāh, S. Arabia 21 C4
l Mawsil, Iraq 21 B3
l Qatif, S. Arabia 21 C3
labama, □ U.S.A. 37 D9
lagôas, □ Brazil 41 E11
lagoinhas, Brazil 41 F11
land, Fin. 17 F16
laska, □ U.S.A. 34 B4
lba Iulia, Rom. 11 E11
lbacete, Spain 13 C5
lbania, ■ Europe 15 D9
lbany, U.S.A. 37 B12
lberta, □ Canada 34 C8
lborg, Den. 17 H10
lbuquerque, U.S.A. 36 C5
ldabra Is., Africa 29 F8
lderney, Channel Is. 12 B4
ldershot, U.K. 7 F7
leppo = Halab, Syria 21 B2
lessándria, Italy 14 B3
lesund, Norw. 16 E9
leutian Is., U.S.A. 34 C2
lexandria = El Iskandarîya, Egypt 31 B10
lfreton, U.K. 6 D6
lgarve, □ Port. 13 D1

Alger, Algeria 30 A5
Algeria, ■ Africa 30 C5
Algiers = Alger, Algeria 30 A5
Alicante, Spain 13 C5
Alice Springs, Australia 26 C5
Alkmaar, Neth. 10 B2
Allahabad, India 22 C5
Allentown, U.S.A. 37 B11
Alloa, U.K. 8 E5
Alma Ata, Kazakhstan 18 E8
Almeria, Spain 13 D4
Alps, Europe 12 D7
Alsace, □ France 12 B7
Altona, Ger. 10 B4
Älvsborg, □ Swed. 17 G12
Amagasaki, Japan 24 B4
Amapá, □ Brazil 41 C8
Amarillo, U.S.A. 36 C6
Amazonas, ≈ S. Amer. 41 D8
Amazonas, □ Brazil 40 D5
Amiens, France 12 B5
Ammän, Jordan 21 B2
Amritsar, India 22 B3
Amsterdam, Neth. 10 B2
Amundsen Gulf, Canada 34 A7
An Najaf, Iraq 21 C3
Anaheim, U.S.A. 36 D3
Anápolis, Brazil 41 G9
Anchorage, Alaska 34 B5
Ancohuma, Bolivia 40 G5
Ancona, Italy 14 C5
Andalucía, □ Spain 13 D3
Andaman Is., Ind. Ocean 22 F7
Andes, Cord. de los, S. Amer. 40 G4
Andhra Pradesh, □ India 22 E4
Andorra, ■ Europe 13 A6
Andria, Italy 14 D7
Andros, Greece 15 F11
Andros I., W. Indies 39 C9
Angers, France 12 C3
Anglesey, U.K. 6 D3
Angola, ■ Africa 33 G3
Angoulême, France 12 D4
Angoumois, □ France 12 D3
Anguilla, W. Indies 38 J19
Anjou, □ France 12 C3
Ankara, Turkey 21 B2
Annaba, Algeria 30 A6
Anshan, China 25 B7
Antananarivo, Madagascar 33 H9
Anticosti, Î. d', Canada 35 D13
Antigua & Barbuda, ■ W. Indies 38 K20
Antofagasta, Chile 42 A2
Antrim, U.K. 9 B5
Antwerpen, Belgium 10 C2
Aomori, Japan 24 F11
Apeldoorn, Neth. 10 B2
Appalachian Mts., U.S.A. 37 C10
Appennini, Italy 14 C3
Ar Ramadi, Iraq 21 B3
Ar Riyāḍ, S. Arabia 21 C3
Arabian Sea, Asia 21 D6
Aracaju, Brazil 41 F11
Arad, Rom. 11 E10
Aragón, □ Spain 13 B5
Arāk, Iran 21 B3
Aral Sea = Aralskoye More, Asia 18 E6
Aralskoye More, Asia 18 E6
Arbil, Iraq 21 B3
Arbroath, U.K. 8 E6
Arctic Ocean 3 A10
Ardabil, Iran 21 B3
Ardennes, Belgium 10 C2

Ardgour, U.K. 8 E3
Arenal, Spain 13 C7
Arequipa, Peru 40 G4
Argentina, ■ S. Amer. 42 E3
Århus, Den. 17 H11
Arizona, □ U.S.A. 36 D4
Arkansas, ≈ U.S.A. 37 C7
Arkansas, □ U.S.A. 37 C6
Arkhangelsk, Russia 18 C5
Arklow, Ire. 9 D5
Armagh, U.K. 9 B5
Armenia, ■ Asia 18 E5
Armenia, Colombia 40 C3
Arnhem, Neth. 10 C2
Arnhem Land, Australia 26 A5
Arran, U.K. 8 F3
Artois, □ France 12 A5
Aru Is., Indonesia 23 D5
Arunachal Pradesh, □ India 22 C7
Asahikawa, Japan 24 F11
Ascension, Atl. Ocean 29 F2
Ascoli Piceno, Italy 14 C5
Ashkhabad, Turkmenistan 18 F6
Asmera, Ethiopia 32 A7
Assam □ India 22 C7
Astrakhan, Russia 18 E5
Asturias, □ Spain 13 A2
Asunción, Paraguay 42 B5
Aswân, Egypt 31 D11
Asyût, Egypt 31 C11
Athabasca, L., Canada 34 C9
Athens = Athínai, Greece 15 F10
Athínai, Greece 15 F10
Athlone, Ire. 9 C4
Atlanta, U.S.A. 37 D10
Atlantic Ocean 2 C7
Auckland, N.Z. 28 G5
Augsburg, Ger. 10 D5
Augusta, U.S.A. 37 D10
Aust-Agder, □ Norw. 17 G9
Austin, U.S.A. 36 D7
Australia, ■ Australasia 26
Australian Alps, Australia 27 F8
Australian Capital Territory, □ Australia 27 F8
Austria, ■ Europe 10 E6
Auvergne, □ France 12 D5
Avellaneda, Argentina 42 C5
Aviemore, U.K. 8 D5
Avignon, France 12 D6
Avila, Spain 13 B3
Avon, □ U.K. 7 F5
Ayers Rock, Australia 26 D5
Ayr, U.K. 8 F4
Azerbaijan, ■ Asia 18 E5
Azores, Atl. Ocean 2 C8
Azovskoye More, Ukraine 18 E4

B

Bâbol, Iran 21 B4
Bacău, Rom. 11 E13
Bacabal, Brazil 41 D10
Badajoz, Spain 13 C2
Badalona, Spain 13 B7
Baden-Württemberg, □ Ger. 10 D4
Badenoch, U.K. 8 E4
Baffin Bay, N. Amer. 35 A13
Baffin I., Canada 35 B12
Baghdād, Iraq 21 B3
Bahamas, ■ W. Indies 39 C9
Bahia, □ Brazil 41 F10
Bahía Blanca, Argentina 42 D4

Bahrain, ■ Asia 21 C4
Baja California, □ Mexico 38 B2
Bakersfield, U.S.A. 36 C3
Bakhtaran, Iran 21 B3
Baku, Azerbaijan 18 E5
Balboa, Panama 38 H14
Baleares, Is., Spain 13 C6
Bali, Indonesia 23 D3
Balkhash, Ozero, Kazakhstan 18 E8
Ballarat, Australia 27 F7
Ballater, U.K. 8 D5
Ballymena, □ U.K. 9 B5
Ballymoney, □ U.K. 9 A5
Balmoral, U.K. 8 D5
Baltic Sea, Europe 17 H15
Baltimore, U.S.A. 37 C11
Bamako, Mali 30 F3
Bamberg, Ger. 10 D5
Banbridge, U.K. 9 B5
Bandon, Ire. 9 E3
Bandung, Indonesia 23 D2
Banff, U.K. 8 D6
Bangalore, India 22 F4
Banghāzī, Libya 31 B9
Bangkok, Thailand 23 B2
Bangladesh, ■ Asia 22 D6
Bangor, U.K. 9 B6
Bangui, Cent. Afr. Rep. 32 D3
Banjarmasin, Indonesia 23 D3
Banks I., Canada 34 A7
Bantry, Ire. 9 E2
Baotou, China 25 B5
Baranof I., Alaska 34 C6
Barbados, ■ W. Indies 38 P22
Barbuda, W. Indies 38 K20
Barcelona, Spain 13 B7
Bardsey I., U.K. 6 E3
Bareilly, India 22 C4
Barents Sea, Arctic 18 B5
Bari, Italy 14 D7
Barkly Tableland, Australia 26 B6
Barletta, Italy 14 D7
Barnsley, U.K. 6 D6
Barquisimeto, Venezuela 40 A5
Barra, U.K. 8 E1
Barrancabermeja, Colombia 40 B4
Barranquilla, Colombia 40 A4
Barrow-in-Furness, U.K. 6 C4
Barry, U.K. 7 F4
Basel, Switz. 10 E3
Basildon, U.K. 7 F8
Basilicata, □ Italy 14 D6
Basingstoke, U.K. 7 F6
Bass Strait, Australia 27 F8
Basse Terre, Guadeloupe 38 L20
Bath, U.K. 7 F5
Baton Rouge, U.S.A. 37 D8
Bauru, Brazil 41 H9
Bayern, □ Ger. 10 D5
Baykal, Ozero, Russia 19 D11
Bayonne, France 12 E3
Bayrūt, Lebanon 21 B2
Beaujolais, France 12 C6
Beaumont, U.S.A. 37 D8
Bedford, U.K. 7 E7
Bedfordshire, □ U.K. 7 E7
Beijing, China 25 C6
Beira, Mozambique 33 H7
Belém, Brazil 41 D9
Belfast, U.K. 9 B6
Belgium, ■ Europe 10 C2
Belgrade = Beograd, Yug. 15 B9

Belize, ■ Cent. Amer. 38 D7
Belmopan, Belize 38 D7
Belo Horizonte, Brazil 41 G10
Belorussia, ■ Europe 18 D3
Beloye More, Russia 18 C4
Ben Nevis, U.K. 8 E4
Benares = Varanasi, India 22 C5
Benbecula, U.K. 8 D1
Bengal, B. of, Ind. Ocean 22 E6
Bengbu, China 25 C6
Benguela, Angola 33 G2
Beni Suef, Egypt 31 C11
Benidorm, Spain 13 C5
Benin, ■ Africa 30 G5
Benin, Bight of, Africa 30 H5
Benin City, Nigeria 30 G6
Benoni, S. Africa 33 K5
Benue, ≈ Africa 30 G6
Benxi, China 25 B7
Beograd, Yug. 15 B9
Bergamo, Italy 14 B3
Bergen, Norw. 17 F8
Bering Sea, Arctic 19 D17
Berkeley, U.S.A. 36 C2
Berkshire, □ U.K. 7 F6
Berlin, Ger. 10 B6
Bermuda, □ Atl. Ocean 39 A12
Bern, Switz. 10 E3
Berwick-upon-Tweed, U.K. 6 B6
Besançon, France 12 C7
Béziers, France 12 E5
Bhopal, India 22 D4
Bhutan, ■ Asia 22 C7
Białystok, Poland 11 B11
Biarritz, France 12 E3
Biel, Switz. 10 E3
Bielefeld, Ger. 10 B4
Bielsko-Biala, Poland 11 D9
Bihar, □ India 22 D6
Bijagos, Arquipélago dos, Guinea-Bissau 30 F1
Bilbao, Spain 13 A4
Billings, U.S.A. 36 A5
Bioko, Eq. Guinea 32 D1
Birkenhead, U.K. 6 D4
Birmingham, U.K. 7 E6
Birmingham, U.S.A. 37 D9
Biscay, B. of, Europe 12 D1
Bishkek, Kirghizia 18 E8
Bishop Auckland, U.K. 6 C6
Bitola, Yug. 15 D9
Biwa-Ko, Japan 24 B5
Black Sea, Europe 18 E4
Blackburn, U.K. 6 D5
Blackpool, U.K. 6 D4
Blanc, Mt., Europe 12 D7
Blantyre, Malawi 33 H7
Blaydon, U.K. 6 C6
Blekinge, □ Swed. 17 H13
Bloemfontein, S. Africa 33 K5
Blue Nile = Nîl el Azraq, ≈ Africa 31 E11
Blyth, U.K. 6 B6
Bobo-Dioulasso, Burkina Faso 30 F4
Bochum, Ger. 10 C3
Boden, Swed. 16 D16
Bodmin Moor, U.K. 7 G3
Boggeragh Mts., Ire. 9 D3
Bogotá, Colombia 40 C4
Böhmerwald, Ger. 10 D6
Bolivia, ■ S. Amer. 40 G5
Bologna, Italy 14 B4
Bolton, U.K. 6 D5
Bombay, India 22 E3

Bonn, Ger. 10 C3
Boothia, Gulf of, Canada 35 A11
Bootle, U.K. 6 D4
Borås, Swed. 17 H12
Bordeaux, France 12 A4
Borders, □ U.K. 8 F5
Borlänge, Swed. 17 F13
Borneo, □ Indonesia 23 C3
Bornholm, Den. 17 J13
Bosnia & Herzegovina, □ Yug. 14 B7
Bosporus, Turkey 21 A1
Boston, U.S.A. 37 B12
Boston, U.K. 6 E7
Bothnia, G. of, Scandinavia 16 E16
Botoşani, Rom. 11 E13
Botswana, ■ Africa 33 J4
Bouaké, Ivory Coast 30 G3
Boulogne, France 12 A4
Bourbonnais, □ France 12 C5
Bourges, France 12 C5
Bournemouth, U.K. 7 G6
Bowland, Forest of, U.K. 6 D5
Boyne, ≈ Ire. 9 C5
Brăila, Rom. 11 F13
Bradford, U.K. 6 D6
Braga, Port. 13 B1
Brahmaputra, ≈ India 22 C7
Brandenburg, Ger. 10 B6
Brantford, Canada 35 D11
Brasília, Brazil 41 G9
Braşov, Rom. 11 F12
Bratislava, Czech. 10 D8
Bratsk, Russia 19 D11
Braunschweig, Ger. 10 B5
Bray, Ire. 9 C5
Brazil, ■ S. Amer. 41 F8
Brazzaville, Congo 32 E3
Breadalbane, U.K. 8 E4
Brecon Beacons, U.K. 7 F4
Breda, Neth. 10 C2
Bremen, Ger. 10 B4
Bremerhaven, Ger. 10 B4
Brentwood, U.K. 7 F8
Bréscia, Italy 14 B4
Bressay, U.K. 8 A7
Brest, France 12 B1
Bretagne, □ France 12 B2
Bridgeport, U.S.A. 37 B12
Bridgetown, Barbados 38 P22
Bridgwater, U.K. 7 F4
Bridlington, U.K. 6 C7
Brighton, U.K. 7 G7
Bríndisi, Italy 15 D7
Brisbane, Australia 27 D9
Bristol, U.K. 7 F5
Bristol Channel, U.K. 7 F3
British Columbia, □ Canada 34 C7
Brno, Czech. 10 D8
Broads, The, U.K. 6 E9
Brooks Range, Alaska 34 B5
Brugge, Belgium 10 C1
Brunei, ■ Asia 23 C3
Brussel, Belgium 10 C2
Bruxelles = Brussel, Belgium 10 C2
Bucaramanga, Colombia 40 B4
Buchan, U.K. 8 D6
Bucharest = Bucureşti, Rom. 11 F13
Buckinghamshire, □ U.K. 7 F7
Bucureşti, Rom. 11 F13
Budapest, Hungary 11 E9
Buenaventura, Colombia 40 C3
Buenos Aires, Argentina 42 C5
Buffalo, U.S.A. 37 B11
Buga, Colombia 40 C3
Bujumbura, Burundi 32 E5
Bukavu, Zaïre 32 E5
Bulawayo, Zimbabwe 33 J5
Bulgaria, ■ Europe 15 C11
Bûr Saîd, Egypt 31 B11
Bûr Sûdân, Sudan 31 E12
Burgas, Bulg. 15 C12
Burgenland, □ Austria 10 E8
Burgos, Spain 13 A4
Burkina Faso, ■ Africa 30 F4
Burma, ■ Asia 22 D8
Bursa, Turkey 21 A1
Burton-on-Trent, U.K. 6 E6
Buru, Indonesia 23 D4
Burundi, ■ Africa 32 E5
Buskerud, □ Norw. 17 F10
Bute, U.K. 8 F3
Bydgoszcz, Poland 11 B8
Bylot I., Canada 35 A12
Bytom, Poland 11 C9

C

Cabimas, Venezuela 40 A4
Cabinda, □ Angola 32 F2
Cáceres, Spain 13 C2
Cádiz, Spain 13 D2
Caen, France 12 B3
Caernarfon B., U.K. 6 D3
Cágliari, Italy 14 E3
Caha Mts., Ire. 9 E2
Cairngorm Mts., U.K. 8 D5
Cairo = El Qâhira, Egypt 31 B11
Calabar, Nigeria 30 G6
Calábria, □ Italy 14 E7

Calais, France 12 A4
Calcutta, India 22 D6
Calgary, Canada 34 C8
Cali, Colombia 40 C3
Calicut, India 22 F4
California, □ U.S.A. 36 C2
Callao, Peru 40 F3
Caltanissetta, Italy 14 F5
Camagüey, Cuba 39 C9
Cambodia, ■ Asia 23 B2
Camborne, U.K. 7 G2
Cambrian Mts., U.K. 7 E4
Cambridge, U.K. 7 E8
Cambridgeshire, □ U.K. 7 E8
Camden, U.S.A. 37 C12
Cameroon, ■ Africa 32 C2
Cameroon, Mt., Cameroon 32 D1
Campania, □ Italy 14 D6
Campbeltown, U.K. 8 F3
Campeche, G. de, Mexico 38 D6
Campina Grande, Brazil 41 E11
Campinas, Brazil 41 H9
Campo Grande, Brazil 41 H8
Campos, Brazil 41 H10
Canada, ■ N. Amer. 34 C10
Canarias, Is., Atl. Ocean 30 C1
Canaveral, C., U.S.A. 37 E10
Canberra, Australia 27 F8
Cannes, France 12 E7
Canouan, W. Indies 38 Q20
Cantabria, □ Spain 13 A3
Canterbury, U.K. 7 F9
Canton = Guangzhou, China 25 D6
Cape Province, □ S. Africa 33 L4
Cape Town, S. Africa 33 L3
Cape York Pen., Australia 27 A7
Caprivi Strip, Namibia 33 H4
Caracas, Venezuela 40 A5
Caratinga, Brazil 41 G10
Cardiff, U.K. 7 F4
Cardigan B., U.K. 7 E3
Carlisle, U.K. 6 C5
Carlow, Ire. 9 D5
Carmarthen B., U.K. 7 F3
Carnegie, L., Australia 26 D3
Caroline Is., Pac. Ocean 3 D17
Carpathians, Europe 11 E12
Carpentaria, Gulf of, Australia 27 A6
Carrara, Italy 14 B4
Carrickfergus, U.K. 9 B6
Cartagena, Spain 13 D5
Cartagena, Colombia 40 A3
Cartago, Colombia 40 C3
Caruaru, Brazil 41 E11
Carúpano, Venezuela 40 A6
Casablanca, Morocco 30 B3
Caspian Sea, Asia 18 E6
Castellón de la Plana, Spain 13 C5
Castilla - La Mancha, □ Spain 13 C3
Castilla y Leon, □ Spain 13 B3
Castries, St. Lucia 38 N21
Cataluña, □ Spain 13 B6
Catánia, Italy 14 F6
Catanzaro, Italy 14 E7
Cavan, □ Ire. 9 B4
Caviana, I., Brazil 41 C9
Ceara, □ Brazil 41 E11
Cebu, Philippines 23 B4
Cedar L., Canada 34 C10
Celebes Sea, Asia 23 C4
Celebes = Sulawesi, Indonesia 23 D4
Central, □ U.K. 8 E4
Central African Rep., ■ Africa 32 C4
Central America, ■ 38 E7
Ceram, Indonesia 23 D4
Cerignola, Italy 14 D6
Ceylon = Sri Lanka, ■ Asia 22 G5
Chad, ■ Africa 31 E8
Champagne, □ France 12 B6
Chang, ≈ China 25 C7
Changchun, China 25 B7
Changsha, China 25 D6
Changzhou, China 25 C7
Channel Is., U.K. 12 B2
Charleston, U.S.A. 37 D10
Charlotte, U.S.A. 37 C10
Charlottenburg, Ger. 10 B6
Charlottetown, Canada 35 D13
Chatham, U.K. 7 F8
Chattanooga, U.S.A. 37 C9
Cheju Do, S. Korea 25 C7
Chelmsford, U.K. 7 F8
Cheltenham, U.K. 7 F5
Chelyabinsk, Russia 18 D7
Chemnitz, Ger. 10 C6
Chengdu, China 25 C5
Cherbourg, France 12 B3
Cheremkhovo, Russia 19 D11
Chesapeake B., U.S.A. 37 C11
Cheshire, □ U.K. 6 D5
Chester, U.K. 6 D5
Chesterfield, U.K. 6 D6
Cheviot Hills, U.K. 6 B5
Chiba, Japan 23 B7
Chicago, U.S.A. 37 B9
Chichagof I., Alaska 34 C6
Chiclayo, Peru 40 E3
Chihuahua, Mexico 38 B3
Chile, ■ S. Amer. 42 D2

Chiloe I. de, Chile 42 E2
Chiltern Hills, U.K. 7 F7
Chimborazo, Ecuador 40 D3
China, ■ Asia 25 C4
Chingola, Zambia 33 G5
Chita, Russia 19 D12
Chittagong, Bangladesh 22 D7
Chongqing, China 25 D5
Chonos, Arch. de los, Chile 42 E2
Chorzów, Poland 11 C9
Christchurch, N.Z. 28 K4
Christmas I., Australia 23 E2
Chukotskoye More, Russia 19 C19
Chungking = Chongqing, China 25 D5
Ciénaga, Colombia 40 A4
Cienfuegos, Cuba 39 C8
Cincinnati, U.S.A. 37 C10
Ciudad Bolivar, Venezuela 40 B6
Ciudad Guayana, Venezuela 40 B6
Ciudad Juárez, Mexico 38 A3
Ciudad Real, Spain 13 C4
Clacton, U.K. 7 F9
Clare, □ Ire. 9 D2
Cleethorpes, U.K. 6 D7
Clermont-Ferrand, France 12 D5
Cleveland, U.S.A. 37 B10
Cleveland, □ U.K. 6 C6
Clonmel, Ire. 9 D4
Cluj-Napoca, Rom. 11 E11
Clwyd, □ U.K. 6 D4
Clyde, ≈ U.K. 8 F5
Clyde, Firth of, U.K. 8 F3
Clydebank, U.K. 8 F4
Coalville, U.K. 6 E6
Coast Ranges, U.S.A. 36 C2
Coatbridge, U.K. 8 F4
Coats I., Canada 35 B11
Cobh, Ire. 9 E3
Cochabamba, Bolivia 40 G5
Cocos or Keeling Is., Australia 23 E1
Coimbra, Port. 13 B1
Colchester, U.K. 7 F8
Coleraine, □ U.K. 9 A5
Coll, U.K. 8 E2
Cologne = Köln, Ger. 10 C3
Colombia, ■ S. Amer. 40 C4
Colombo, Sri Lanka 22 G5
Colón, Panama 38 H14
Colonsay, U.K. 8 E2
Colorado, □ U.S.A. 36 C5
Colorado, ≈ U.S.A. 36 D4
Colorado Springs, U.S.A. 36 C6
Columbia, ≈ U.S.A. 36 A2
Columbia, U.S.A. 37 D10
Columbus, Georgia, U.S.A. 37 D10
Columbus, Ohio, U.S.A. 37 C10
Colwyn Bay, U.K. 6 D4
Comeragh Mts., Ire. 9 D4
Como, Italy 14 B3
Comoros, ■ Africa 29 G8
Conakry, Guinea 30 G2
Concepcion, Chile 42 D2
Congo, ■ Africa 32 E3
Congo = Zaïre, ≈ Africa 32 D4
Connacht, Ire. 9 C2
Connecticut, □ U.S.A. 37 B12
Connemara, Ire. 9 C2
Constanţa, Rom. 11 F14
Constantine, Algeria 30 A6
Cookstown, U.K. 9 B5
Cooper Creek, ≈ Australia 27 D6
Copenhagen = København, Den. 17 J12
Córdoba, Spain 13 D3
Córdoba, Argentina 42 C4
Corfu = Kérkira, Greece 15 E8
Cork, Ire. 9 E3
Cornwall, □ U.K. 7 G3
Coronation Gulf, Canada 34 B8
Corpus Christi, U.S.A. 36 E7
Corse, France 14 C3
Corsica = Corse, France 14 C3
Cosenza, Italy 14 E7
Costa Blanca, Spain 13 C5
Costa Brava, Spain 13 B7
Costa del Sol, Spain 13 D4
Costa Dorada, Spain 13 B7
Costa Rica, ■ Cent. Amer. 39 F8
Cote d'Ivoire = Ivory Coast,
■ Africa 30 G3
Cotonou, Benin 30 G5
Cotopaxi, Ecuador 40 D3
Cotswold Hills, U.K. 7 F6
Cottbus, Ger. 10 C7
Coventry, U.K. 7 E6
Craiova, Rom. 11 F11
Crawley, U.K. 7 F7
Cremona, Italy 14 B4
Crete = Kríti, Greece 15 G11
Crewe, U.K. 6 D5
Croatia, ■ Europe 14 B6
Cromarty, U.K. 8 D4
Cuba, ■ W. Indies 39 C8
Cúcuta, Colombia 40 B4
Cuenca, Ecuador 40 D3
Cuenca, Spain 13 B4
Cuiaba, Brazil 41 G7
Cumaná, Venezuela 40 A6
Cumbernauld, U.K. 8 F4

Cumbria, □ U.K. 6 C5
Cumbrian Mts., U.K. 6 C4
Curaçao, Neth. Ant. 40 A5
Curitiba, Brazil 42 B7
Cuzco, Peru 40 F4
Cwmbran, U.K. 7 F4
Cyclades = Kikládhes, Greece 15 F11
Cyprus, ■ Asia 21 B2
Czech Rep., □ Czech. 10 D7
Czechoslovakia, ■ Europe 10 D8
Czestochowa, Poland 11 C9

D

Dakar, Senegal 30 F1
Dalian, China 25 C7
Dallas, U.S.A. 37 D7
Damaraland, Namibia 33 J3
Damascus = Dimashq, Syria 21 B2
Dandong, China 25 B7
Danube = Dunarea, ≈ Europe 11 F14
Dar-es-Salaam, Tanzania 32 F7
Dardanelles, Turkey 21 A1
Darién, G. del, S. Amer. 40 B3
Darling, ≈ Australia 27 E7
Darlington, U.K. 6 C6
Darmstadt, Ger. 10 D4
Dartmoor, U.K. 7 G4
Dartmouth, Canada 35 D13
Darwin, Australia 26 A5
Datong, China 25 B6
Dauphine, □ France 12 D6
Davao, Philippines 23 C4
Davis Str., N. Amer. 35 B14
Dayton, U.S.A. 37 C10
Dead Sea, Asia 21 B2
Deal, U.K. 7 F9
Dean, Forest of, U.K. 7 F5
Debrecen, Hungary 11 E10
Delaware, □ U.S.A. 37 C11
Delhi, India 22 C4
Denmark, ■ Europe 17 J10
Denver, U.S.A. 36 C6
Derby, U.K. 6 E6
Derbyshire, □ U.K. 6 D6
Derryveagh Mts., Ire. 9 A4
Des Moines, U.S.A. 37 B8
Dessau, Ger. 10 C6
Detroit, U.S.A. 37 B10
Devon, □ U.K. 7 G4
Devon I., Canada 35 A11
Dezfül, Iran 21 B3
Dhaka, Bangladesh 22 D7
Dhodhekanisos, Greece 15 F12
Dieppe, France 12 B4
Dijon, France 12 C6
Dimashq, Syria 21 B2
Dingle B., Ire. 9 D1
Dingwall, U.K. 8 D4
Disappointment, L., Australia 26 C3
Diyarbakir, Turkey 21 B3
Dnepropetrovsk, Ukraine 18 E4
Dolomiti, Italy 14 A4
Dominica, ■ W. Indies 38 M20
Dominican Rep., ■ W. Indies 39 D10
Don, ≈ Russia 18 E5
Doncaster, U.K. 6 D6
Donegal, Ire. 9 B3
Donetsk, Ukraine 18 E4
Dordrecht, Neth. 10 C2
Dornoch, U.K. 8 D4
Dorset, □ U.K. 7 G5
Dortmund, Ger. 10 C3
Douala, Cameroon 32 D1
Dounreay, U.K. 8 C5
Douro, ≈ Port. 13 B1
Dover, U.K. 7 F9
Down, □ U.K. 9 B6
Drakensberg, S. Africa 33 K5
Drammen, Norw. 17 G11
Dresden, Ger. 10 C6
Drogheda, Ire. 9 C5
Dublin, Ire. 9 C5
Dubrovnik, Yug. 15 C8
Dudley, U.K. 7 E5
Duisburg, Ger. 10 C3
Duluth, U.S.A. 37 A8
Dumbarton, U.K. 8 F4
Dumfries, U.K. 8 F5
Dumfries and Galloway, □ U.K. 8 F5
Dumyât, Egypt 31 B11
Dun Laoghaire, Ire. 9 C5
Dunarea, ≈ Europe 11 F14
Dundalk, Ire. 9 B5
Dundee, U.K. 8 E6
Dunedin, N.Z. 28 L3
Dunfermline, U.K. 8 E5
Dungannon, U.K. 9 B5
Dungarvan, Ire. 9 D4
Dunkerque, France 12 A5
Durango, Mexico 38 C4
Durban, S. Africa 33 K6
Durham, □ U.K. 6 C6
Dushanbe, Tajikistan 18 F7
Düsseldorf, Ger. 10 C3
Dyfed, □ U.K. 7 E3

E

East China Sea, Asia 25
East Kilbride, U.K. 8
East London, S. Africa 33
East Siberian Sea, Arctic ....19 B
East Sussex, □ U.K. 7
Eastbourne, U.K. 7
Easter Is., Pac. Ocean 2
Ebbw Vale, U.K. 7
Ebro, ≈ Spain 13
Ech Cheliff, Algeria 30
Ecuador, ■ S. Amer. 40
Eday, U.K. 8
Edinburgh, U.K. 8
Edmonton, Canada 34
Edward, L., Africa 32
Egypt, ■ Africa ....31 D
Eifel, Ger. 10
Eigg, U.K. 8
Eighty Mile Beach, Australia 26
Eindhoven, Neth. 10
El Faiyûm, Egypt ....31 C
El Ferrol, Spain 13
El Gîza, Egypt ....31 C
El Iskandarîya, Egypt ....31 C
El Khartûm, Sudan ....31 E
El Mahalla el Kubra, Egypt ....31 B
El Mansûra, Egypt ....31 B
El Minyâ, Egypt ....31 C
El Obeid, Sudan ....31 F
El Paso, U.S.A. ....36 D
El Qâhira, Egypt ....31 B
El Salvador, ■ Cent. Amer. 38
El Suweis, Egypt ....31 C
Elba, Italy ....14 C
Elbe, ≈ Ger. ....10 B
Elblag, Poland ....11 B
Elburz Mts., Iran 21
Elche, Spain ....13 C
Eleuthera I., W. Indies 39
Elgin, U.K. 8
Ellesmere Port, U.K. 6
Emilia Romagna, □ Italy 14
England, □ U.K. 7
English Channel, Europe 7
Ennis, Ire. 9
Enniscorthy, Ire. 9
Enschede, Neth. 10
Enugu, Nigeria 30
Equatorial Guinea, ■ Africa 32
Erawadi Myit, ≈ Burma 22
Erfurt, Ger. 10
Erie, L., N. Amer. ....35 D
Eritrea, □ Ethiopia 32
Erzurum, Turkey 21
Esbjerg, Den. ....17 J
Esfahân, Iran 21
Eskilstuna, Swed. ....17 G
Eskisehir, Turkey 21
Espírito Santo, □ Brazil 41 G1
Essen, Ger. ....10 C
Essex, □ U.K. 7
Estonia, ■ Europe ....18 D
Ethiopia, ■ Africa 32
Etna, Mt., Italy 14
Euphrates, ≈ Asia 21
Evansville, U.S.A. 37
Everest, Mt., Nepal 22
Everglades, U.S.A. 37 E1
Évora, Port. 13
Évvoia, Greece 15 E1
Exeter, U.K. 7
Exmoor, U.K. 7
Extremadura, □ Spain 13
Eyre, L., Australia 27
Eyre Peninsula, Australia 26

F

Fairbanks, Alaska ....34 B
Falkirk, U.K. 8
Falkland Is., Atl. Ocean ....42 G
Fareham, U.K. 7
Farnborough, U.K. 7
Faroe Is., Atl. Ocean 5
Feira de Santana, Brazil 41 F1
Fens, The, U.K. 6
Fermanagh, □ U.K. 9
Ferrara, Italy ....14 B
Fès, Morocco ....30 B
Fetlar, U.K. ....8 A
Fife, □ U.K. ....8 E
Fiji, ■ Pac. Ocean ....28 C
Finland, ■ Europe 16 C11
Finnmark, □ Norw. 16 B1
Firenze, Italy ....14 C
Flandre, Belgium ....10 C
Fleetwood, U.K. ....6 D
Flensburg, Ger. ....10 A
Flinders I., Australia ....27 F
Flint, U.S.A. 37 B10
Florence = Firenze, Italy ....14 C
Flores, Indonesia ....23 D
Florida, □ U.S.A. 37 E1
Fóggia, Italy ....14 D
Folkestone, U.K. 7 F9
Fort de France, Martinique 38 N20
Fort Smith, U.S.A. 37

CALIFORNIA.

rt Wayne, U.S.A. ...37 B9
rt William, U.K. ...8 E3
rt Worth, U.S.A. ...36 D7
rtaleza, Brazil ...41 D11
rth, Firth of, U.K. ...8 E6
oula, U.K. ...8 A6
oxe Channel, Canada ...35 B11
rance, ■ Europe ...12 C4
anche-Comte, □ France ...12 C6
ankfurt am Main, Ger. ...10 C4
ankfurt an der Oder, Ger. ...10 B7
änkische Alb, Ger. ...10 D5
raser I., Australia ...27 D9
raserburgh, U.K. ...8 D6
rederikshavn, Den. ...17 H11
rederikstad, Norw. ...17 G11
reetown, Sierra Leone ...30 G2
reiburg, Ger. ...10 D3
rench Guiana, ■ S. Amer. ...41 C8
resno, U.S.A. ...36 C3
riuli Venezia Giulia, □ Italy ...14 A5
rome, L., Australia ...27 E6
runze = Bishkek, Kirghizia ...18 E8
uji-San, Japan ...24 B6
ukuoka, Japan ...24 C2
ukushima, Japan ...24 G11
unabashi, Japan ...24 B7
urneaux Group, Australia ...27 G8
ürth, Ger. ...10 D5
ushun, China ...25 B7
uzhou, China ...25 D6
yn, Den. ...17 J11

G
Gabon, ■ Africa ...32 E2
Gaborone, Botswana ...33 J5
Gairdner, L., Australia ...26 E6
Galaţi, Rom. ...11 F14
Galapagos Is., ≈ Pac. Ocean ...2 E5
Galashiels, U.K. ...8 F6
Galicia, □ Spain ...13 A1
Gällivare, Swed. ...16 C16
Galloway, U.K. ...8 G4
Galveston, U.S.A. ...37 E8
Galway, Ire. ...9 C2
Gambia, ■ Africa ...30 F1
Gamboa, Panama ...38 H14
Ganga, ≈ Ind./Bangla. ...22 C4
Ganges = Ganga, ≈ Ind./Bangla. ...22 C4
Gaoxiong, Taiwan ...25 D7
Garda, L. di, Italy ...14 B4
Gary, U.S.A. ...37 B9
Gascogne, □ France ...12 E3
Gaspé, Pén de, Canada ...35 D13
Gateshead, U.K. ...6 C6
Gatun, Panama ...38 H14
Gävle, Swed. ...17 F14
Gävleborg, □ Swed. ...17 F14
Gaza, Israel ...21 B2
Gaziantep, Turkey ...21 B2
Gdansk, Poland ...11 A9
Gdynia, Poland ...11 A9
Geelong, Australia ...27 F7
Gelsenkirchen, Ger. ...10 C3
Genève, Switz. ...10 E3
Gênova, Italy ...14 B3
Gent, Belgium ...10 C1
George Town, Malaysia ...23 C2
Georgetown, Guyana ...40 B7
Georgia, ■ Asia ...18 E5
Georgia, □ U.S.A. ...37 D10
Gera, Ger. ...10 C6
Germany, ■ Europe ...10 C5
Germiston, S. Africa ...33 K5
Gerona, Spain ...13 B7
Ghana, ■ Africa ...30 G4
Giant's Causeway, U.K. ...9 A5
Gibraltar, □ Europe ...13 D3
Gibson Desert, Australia ...26 C3
Gifu, Japan ...24 B5
Gigha, U.K. ...8 F3
Gijón, Spain ...13 A3
Gillingham, U.K. ...7 F8
Gisborne, N.Z. ...28 H7
Gjøvik, Norw. ...17 F11
Glasgow, U.K. ...8 F4
Glendale, U.S.A. ...36 D3
Glenrothes, U.K. ...8 E5
Gliwice, Poland ...11 C9
Glogów, Poland ...10 C8
Gloucester, U.K. ...7 F5
Gloucestershire, □ U.K. ...7 F5
Goa, □ India ...22 E3
Goiânia, Brazil ...41 G9
Goias, □ Brazil ...41 F9
Good Hope, C. of, S. Africa ...33 L3
Gorkiy = Nizhniy Novgorod, Russia ...18 D5
Gorlitz, Ger. ...10 C7
Gosport, U.K. ...7 G6
Göteborg, Swed. ...17 H14
Gotland, Swed. ...17 H15
Götaland, Swed. ...17 G12
Gozo, Malta ...14 F14
Grampian, □ U.K. ...8 D6
Grampian Highlands, U.K. ...8 E4
Gran Canaria, Canary Is. ...30 C1
Granada, Spain ...13 D4
Grand Bahama I., W. Indies ...39 B9

Grand Canyon, U.S.A. ...36 C4
Grand Cayman, W. Indies ...39 D8
Grand Rapids, U.S.A. ...37 B9
Grangemouth, U.K. ...8 E5
Grantham, U.K. ...6 E7
Gravesend, U.K. ...7 F8
Graz, Austria ...10 E7
Great Abaco I., W. Indies ...39 B9
Great Australian Bight, Australia ...26 E4
Great Barrier Reef, Australia ...27 B8
Great Bear L., Canada ...34 B7
Great Divide, Australia ...27 C8
Great Falls, U.S.A. ...36 A4
Great Inagua I., W. Indies ...39 C10
Great Salt Lake, U.S.A. ...36 B4
Great Sandy Desert, Australia ...26 C3
Great Slave L., Canada ...34 B8
Great Victoria Desert, Australia ...26 D4
Great Wall, The, China ...25 C5
Great Yarmouth, U.K. ...6 E9
Greater Antilles, W. Indies ...39 D9
Greater Manchester, □ U.K. ...6 D5
Greece, ■ Europe ...15 E9
Green Bay, U.S.A. ...37 B9
Greenland, ■ N. Amer. ...35 B15
Greenock, U.K. ...8 F4
Greensboro, U.S.A. ...37 C11
Grenada, ■ W. Indies ...38 Q20
Grenoble, France ...12 D6
Gretna Green, U.K. ...8 F5
Grey Range, Australia ...27 D7
Grimsby, U.K. ...6 D7
Groningen, Neth. ...10 B3
Groot Karoo, S. Africa ...33 L4
Groote Eylandt, Australia ...27 A6
Gross Glockner, Austria ...10 E6
Grudziadz, Poland ...11 B9
Guadalajara, Mexico ...38 C4
Guadalajara, Spain ...13 B4
Guadarrama, Sierra de, Spain ...13 B4
Guadeloupe, □ W. Indies ...38 L20
Guadiana, ≈ Port. ...13 D2
Guadix, Spain ...13 D4
Guangzhou, China ...25 D6
Guantanamo, Cuba ...39 C9
Guatemala, ■ Cent. Amer. ...38 D6
Guatemala City, Guatemala ...38 E6
Guayaquil, Ecuador ...40 D2
Guelph, Canada ...35 D11
Guernsey, Channel Is. ...12 B2
Guildford, U.K. ...7 F7
Guinea, ■ Africa ...30 F2
Guinea-Bissau, ■ Africa ...30 F1
Guiyang, China ...25 D5
Gujarat, □ India ...22 D3
Gulf, The, Asia ...21 C4
Guyana, ■ S. Amer. ...40 B7
Guyenne, □ France ...12 D4
Gwalior, India ...22 C4
Gwent, □ U.K. ...7 F4
Gwynedd, □ U.K. ...6 E4
Györ, Hungary ...11 E8

H
Haarlem, Neth. ...10 B2
Hachinohe, Japan ...24 F11
Hadrian's Wall, U.K. ...6 C5
Hagen, Ger. ...10 C3
Haifa, Israel ...21 B2
Hainan Dao, China ...25 E6
Haiti, ■ W. Indies ...39 D10
Hakodate, Japan ...24 F11
Halab, Syria ...21 B2
Halberstadt, Ger. ...10 C5
Halifax, Canada ...35 D13
Halifax, U.K. ...6 D6
Halland, □ Swed. ...17 H12
Halle, Ger. ...10 C5
Halmstad, Swed. ...17 H12
Hamã, Syria ...21 B2
Hamadān, Iran ...21 B3
Hamamatsu, Japan ...24 B5
Hamar, Norw. ...17 F11
Hamburg, Ger. ...10 B5
Hame, □ Fin. ...17 F17
Hameln, Ger. ...10 B4
Hamilton, N.Z. ...28 G5
Hamilton, U.K. ...8 F4
Hamilton, Canada ...35 D11
Hamm, Ger. ...10 C3
Hammerfest, Norw. ...16 A17
Hammond, U.S.A. ...37 B9
Hampshire, □ U.K. ...7 F6
Hangzhou, China ...25 C6
Hannover, Ger. ...10 B4
Hanoi, Vietnam ...23 A2
Harare, Zimbabwe ...33 H6
Harbin, China ...25 B7
Harlow, U.K. ...7 F8
Härnösand, Swed. ...16 E15
Harrogate, U.K. ...6 D6
Hartlepool, U.K. ...6 C6
Haryana, □ India ...22 C4
Hastings, N.Z. ...28 H6
Hastings, U.K. ...7 G8
Haugesund, Norw. ...17 G8
Haut Atlas, Morocco ...30 B4
Havana = La Habana, Cuba ...39 C8

Havant, U.K. ...7 G7
Hawaii, Pac. Ocean ...2 C2
Hawaii, □ U.S.A. ...36 H16
Hawick, U.K. ...8 F6
Hedmark, □ Norw. ...17 F11
Hefei, China ...25 C6
Heidelberg, Ger. ...10 D4
Heilbronn, Ger. ...10 D4
Helmsdale, U.K. ...8 C5
Helsingborg, Swed. ...17 H12
Helsingor, Den. ...17 H12
Helsinki, Fin. ...17 F18
Hemel Hempstead, U.K. ...7 F7
Hengyang, China ...25 D6
Herat, Afghan. ...21 B5
Hereford, U.K. ...7 E5
Hereford & Worcester, □ U.K. ...7 E5
Herford, Ger. ...10 B4
Hermosillo, Mexico ...38 B2
Hertfordshire, □ U.K. ...7 F7
Hessen, □ Ger. ...10 C4
Higashiōsaka, Japan ...24 B4
High Wycombe, U.K. ...7 F7
Highland, □ U.K. ...8 D4
Hildesheim, Ger. ...10 B4
Hilversum, Neth. ...10 B2
Himachal Pradesh, □ India ...22 B4
Himalaya, Asia ...22 C5
Himeji, Japan ...24 B4
Hims, Syria ...21 B2
Hindu Kush, Afghan. ...21 B5
Hirosaki, Japan ...24 F11
Hiroshima, Japan ...24 B3
Hobart, Australia ...27 G8
Hohhot, China ...25 B6
Hokkaido, Japan ...24 F11
Holderness, U.K. ...6 D7
Holguin, Cuba ...39 C9
Hollywood, U.S.A. ...36 D3
Honduras, ■ Cent. Amer. ...38 E7
Hønefoss, Norw. ...17 F11
Hong Kong, ≈ Asia ...25 D6
Honolulu, Hawaii ...36 H16
Honshu, Japan ...24 B4
Hordaland, □ Norw. ...17 F9
Hormuz, Str. of, Asia ...21 C4
Horn, C. = Hornos, C. de, Chile ...42 H3
Hornos, C. de, Chile ...42 H3
Horsens, Den. ...17 J10
Hospitalet, Spain ...13 B7
Houghton-le-Spring, U.K. ...6 C6
Houston, U.S.A. ...37 E7
Howrah, India ...22 D7
Hoy, U.K. ...8 C5
Hradec Kralove, Czech. ...10 C7
Huainan, China ...25 C6
Huang, ≈ China ...25 C6
Huascarán, Peru ...40 E3
Huddersfield, U.K. ...6 D6
Hudson Bay, Canada ...35 B11
Hudson Str., Canada ...35 B12
Huelva, Spain ...13 D2
Huesca, Spain ...13 A5
Hull, U.K. ...6 D7
Humber, ≈ U.K. ...6 D7
Humberside, □ U.K. ...6 D7
Hungary, ■ Europe ...11 E9
Hunsrück, Ger. ...10 D3
Huron, L., N. Amer. ...37 B10
Hyderabad, India ...22 E4
Hyderabad, Pak. ...22 C2

I
Iaşi, Rom. ...11 E13
Ibadan, Nigeria ...30 G5
Ibagué, Colombia ...40 C3
Ibiza, Spain ...13 C6
Iceland, ■ Europe ...16 D4
Ichinomiya, Japan ...24 B5
Idaho, □ U.S.A. ...36 B3
Île-de-France, □ France ...12 B5
Ikaría, Greece ...15 F12
Illinois, □ U.S.A. ...37 B9
Ilorin, Nigeria ...30 G5
Imphal, India ...22 D7
Inch'on, S. Korea ...25 C7
India, ■ Asia ...22 H3
Indian Ocean, ...22 H3
Indiana, □ U.S.A. ...37 C9
Indianapolis, U.S.A. ...37 C9
Indonesia, ■ Asia ...23 D3
Indore, India ...22 D4
Indus, ≈ Pakistan ...22 C2
Ingolstadt, Ger. ...10 D5
Inishowen Pen., Ire. ...8 D4
Inner Hebrides, U.K. ...8 D2
Innsbruck, Austria ...10 E5
Inveraray, U.K. ...8 E3
Invercargill, N.Z. ...28 M2
Invergordon, U.K. ...8 D4
Inverness, U.K. ...8 D4
Iona, U.K. ...8 E2
Ionian Sea, Europe ...15 E9
Iónioi Nisoi, □ Greece ...15 E9
Iowa, □ U.S.A. ...37 B8
Ípiros, □ Greece ...15 E9
Ipswich, U.K. ...7 E9
Iquique, Chile ...40 H4

Iquitos, Peru ...40 D4
Iráklion, Greece ...15 G11
Iran, ■ Asia ...21 B4
Iraq, ■ Asia ...21 B3
Ireland, ■ Europe ...9 C4
Irian Jaya, □ Indonesia ...23 D5
Irish Sea, Europe ...5 D3
Irkutsk, Russia ...19 D11
Irrawady = Erawadi Myit, ≈ Burma ...22 H9
Irvine, U.K. ...8 F4
Islay, U.K. ...8 F2
Israel, ■ Asia ...21 B2
Istanbul, Turkey ...21 A1
Italy, ■ Europe ...14 C4
Ivory Coast, ■ Africa ...30 G3
Iwaki, Japan ...24 G11
Iwo, Nigeria ...30 G5
Izmir, Turkey ...21 B1

J
Jabalpur, India ...22 D5
Jackson, U.S.A. ...37 D8
Jacksonville, U.S.A. ...37 D10
Jaén, Spain ...13 D4
Jaipur, India ...22 C4
Jakarta, Indonesia ...23 D2
Jamaica, ■ W. Indies ...39 D9
James Bay, Canada ...35 C11
Jammu & Kashmir, □ India ...22 B3
Jämtland, □ Norw. ...16 E13
Japan, ■ Asia ...24 G10
Japan, Sea of, Asia ...24 A3
Java, Indonesia ...23 D2
Jena, Ger. ...10 C5
Jerez, Spain ...13 D2
Jersey, Channel Is. ...12 B2
Jersey City, U.S.A. ...37 B12
Jerusalem, Israel ...21 B2
Jiddah, S. Arabia ...21 C2
Jilin, China ...25 B7
Jilong, Taiwan ...25 D7
Jinan, China ...25 C6
Jinzhou, China ...25 B7
João Pessoa, Brazil ...41 E12
Johannesburg, S. Africa ...33 K5
John O'Groats, U.K. ...8 C5
Johnstone, U.K. ...8 F4
Jönköping, □ Swed. ...17 H12
Jordan, ■ Asia ...21 B2
Juàzeiro do Norte, Brazil ...41 E11
Juiz de Fora, Brazil ...41 H10
Jundiaí, Brazil ...42 A7
Jura, Europe ...12 C6
Jura, U.K. ...8 F3

K
Kabul, Afghan. ...21 B5
Kaduna, Nigeria ...30 F6
Kagoshima, Japan ...24 D2
Kaiserslautern, Ger. ...10 D3
Kalahari, Africa ...3 J4
Kaliningrad, Russia ...18 D3
Kalisz, Poland ...11 C9
Kalmar, □ Swed. ...17 H14
Kamaishi, Japan ...24 G11
Kampala, Uganda ...32 D6
Kampuchea = Cambodia, ■ Asia ...23 B2
Kananga, Zaïre ...32 F4
Kanazawa, Japan ...24 A5
Kandahar, Afghan. ...21 B5
Kangaroo I., Australia ...27 F6
Kano, Nigeria ...30 F6
Kanpur, India ...22 C5
Kansas, □ U.S.A. ...36 C7
Kansas City, U.S.A. ...37 C8
Kaokoveld, Namibia ...33 H2
Kaolack, Senegal ...30 F1
Kara Sea, Arctic ...18 B7
Karachi, Pak. ...22 D2
Karaganda, Kazakhstan ...18 E8
Karbalā, Iraq ...21 B3
Kariba L., Africa ...33 H5
Karlskrona, Swed. ...17 H13
Karlsruhe, Ger. ...10 D4
Karlstad, Swed. ...17 G12
Kärnten, □ Austria ...10 E6
Kárpathos, Greece ...15 G12
Kāshān, Iran ...21 B4
Kassel, Ger. ...10 C4
Katmandu, Nepal ...22 C6
Katowice, Poland ...11 C9
Katsina, Nigeria ...30 F6
Kattegat, Scandinavia ...17 H11
Kawagoe, Japan ...24 B6
Kawasaki, Japan ...24 B6
Kayseri, Turkey ...21 B2
Kazakhstan, ■ Asia ...18 E7
Kazan, Russia ...18 D5
Kecskemét, Hungary ...11 E9
Kefallinia, Greece ...15 E9
Keflavik, Iceland ...16 D1
Keighley, U.K. ...6 D6
Kemān, Iran ...21 B4
Kemi, Fin. ...16 D18
Kenitra, Morocco ...30 B3
Kent, □ U.K. ...7 F8
Kentucky, □ U.S.A. ...37 C9

Kenya, ■ Africa ...32 D7
Kenya, Mt., Kenya ...32 E7
Kerala, □ India ...22 F4
Kérkira, Greece ...15 E8
Kerry, □ Ire. ...9 D2
Keski - Suomen, □ Fin. ...16 E18
Key West, U.S.A. ...37 F10
Khabarovsk, Russia ...19 E14
Kharkov, Ukraine ...18 E4
Khartoum = El Khartûm, Sudan ...31 E11
Khíos, Greece ...15 E11
Khulna, Bangladesh ...22 D6
Kidderminster, U.K. ...7 E5
Kiel, Ger. ...10 A5
Kielce, Poland ...11 C10
Kikládhes, Greece ...15 F11
Kikwit, Zaïre ...32 E3
Kildare, □ Ire. ...9 C5
Kilimanjaro, Tanzania ...32 E7
Kilkenny, □ Ire. ...9 D4
Killarney, Ire. ...9 D2
Kilmarnock, U.K. ...8 F4
Kimberley, Australia ...26 B4
Kimberley, S. Africa ...33 K4
King I., Australia ...27 F7
King William I., Canada ...34 B10
Kings Lynn, U.K. ...6 E8
Kingston, Jamaica ...38 J17
Kingston, U.K. ...7 F7
Kingussie, U.K. ...8 D4
Kinshasa, Zaïre ...32 E3
Kintyre, U.K. ...8 F3
Kirghizia, ■ Asia ...18 E8
Kiribati, ■ Pac. Ocean ...3 D18
Kirkūk, Iraq ...21 B3
Kirkcaldy, U.K. ...8 E5
Kirkwall, U.K. ...8 C6
Kiruna, Swed. ...16 C15
Kisangani, Zaïre ...32 D5
Kishinev, Moldavia ...18 E3
Kitakyūshū, Japan ...24 C2
Kitchener, Canada ...35 D11
Kíthira, Greece ...15 F10
Kitwe, Zambia ...33 G5
Kiva, L., Africa ...32 E5
Kiyev, Ukraine ...18 D4
Klagenfurt, Austria ...10 E7
Knockmealdown Mts., Ire. ...9 D4
Knossos, Greece ...15 G11
Knoxville, U.S.A. ...37 C10
Košice, Czech. ...11 D10
Kobe, Japan ...24 B4
København, Den. ...17 J12
Koblenz, Ger. ...10 C3
Kōchi, Japan ...24 C3
Kodiak I., Alaska ...34 C4
Kolding, Den. ...17 J10
Köln, Ger. ...10 C3
Komsomolsk, Russia ...19 D14
Kongsvinger, Norw. ...17 F12
Konya, Turkey ...21 B2
Kopervik, Norw. ...17 G8
Kopparberg, □ Swed. ...17 F12
Kōriyama, Japan ...24 G11
Kos, Greece ...15 F12
Kosciusko, Mt., Australia ...27 F8
Kowloon, Hong Kong ...25 D6
Kraków, Poland ...11 C9
Krasnodar, Russia ...18 E4
Krasnoyarsk, Russia ...19 D10
Krefeld, Ger. ...10 C3
Kristiansand, Norw. ...17 G10
Kristianstad, □ Swed. ...17 J13
Kristiansund, Norw. ...16 E9
Kriti, Greece ...15 G11
Krivoy Rog, Ukraine ...18 E4
Kronoberg, □ Swed. ...17 H13
Kuala Lumpur, Malaysia ...23 C2
Kumamoto, Japan ...24 C2
Kumasi, Ghana ...30 G4
Kuopio, □ Fin. ...16 E19
Kurashiki, Japan ...24 B3
Kure, Japan ...24 B3
Kurilskiye Ostrova, Russia ...19 E16
Kushiro, Japan ...24 F11
Kuwait, ■ Asia ...21 C3
Kuybyshev = Samara, Russia ...18 D6
Kwangju, S. Korea ...25 C7
Kyūshu, Japan ...24 C2
Kyle of Lochalsh, U.K. ...8 D3
Kyoga, L., Uganda ...32 D6
Kyōto, Japan ...24 B4

L
La Boca, Panama ...38 H14
La Chorrera, Panama ...38 H14
La Coruña, Spain ...13 A1
La Habana, Cuba ...39 C8
La Paz, Bolivia ...40 G5
La Plata, Argentina ...42 D5
La Rioja, □ Spain ...13 A4
La Rochelle, France ...12 C3
La Spézia, Italy ...14 B3
Labrador, Coast of, Canada ...35 C13
Ladozhskoye, Ozero, Russia ...18 C4
Lagos, Port. ...13 D1
Lagos, Nigeria ...30 G5
Lahore, Pak. ...22 B3

Index

Lahti, Fin. 17 F18
Lakshadweep Is., India ...22 F3
Lancashire, □ U.K. 6 D5
Lancaster, U.K. 6 C5
Lancaster Sd., Canada ...35 A11
Landskrona, Swed. 17 J12
Languedoc, □ France 12 E5
Lansing, U.S.A. 37 B10
Lanzhou, China 25 C5
Laois, □ Ire. 9 D4
Laos, ■ Asia 23 B2
Lapi, □ Fin. 16 C19
Lappland, Fin. 16 B18
Laptev Sea, Arctic 19 B13
Laredo, U.S.A. 36 E7
Lárisa, Greece 15 E10
Larne, □ U.K. 9 B6
Las Palmas, Canary Is. ...30 C1
Las Vegas, U.S.A. 36 C3
Latvia, ■ Europe 18 D3
Lauchhammer, Ger. 10 C6
Launceston, Australia 27 G8
Lausanne, Switz. 10 E3
Lawton, U.S.A. 36 D7
Le Havre, France 12 B4
Le Mans, France 12 B4
Le Moule, Guadeloupe 38 L20
Leamington, U.K. 7 E6
Lebanon, ■ Asia 21 B2
Lecce, Italy 15 D8
Leeds, U.K. 6 D6
Leeuwarden, Neth. 10 B2
Leeward Is., W. Indies 39 D12
Legnica, Poland 10 C8
Leicester, U.K. 7 E6
Leicestershire, □ U.K. 7 E6
Leiden, Neth. 10 B2
Leinster, Ire. 9 C4
Leipzig, Ger. 10 C6
Leith, U.K. 8 F5
Leitrim, □ Ire. 9 B3
Lena, ≈ Russia 19 B13
Leningrad = St. Peterburg, Russia ..18 D4
León, Mexico 38 C4
León, Spain 13 A3
Lérida, Spain 13 B6
Lesotho, ■ Africa 33 K5
Lesser Antilles, W. Indies ..39 E12
Lésvos, Greece 15 E11
Letchworth, U.K. 7 F7
Lethbridge, Canada 34 D8
Leuven, Belgium 10 C2
Levkás, Greece 15 E9
Levkôsia, Cyprus 21 B2
Lewis, U.K. 8 C2
Lhasa, China 25 D4
Lianyungang, China 25 C6
Liberec, Czech. 10 C7
Liberia, ■ Africa 30 G3
Lîbîya, Sahrâ, Africa 31 C9
Libreville, Gabon 32 D1
Libya, ■ Africa 31 C8
Liechtenstein, ■ Europe ..10 E4
Liège, Belgium 10 C2
Liffey, ≈ Ire. 9 C5
Liguria, □ Italy 14 B3
Ligurian Sea, Italy 14 C3
Likasi, Zaïre 32 G5
Lille, France 12 A5
Lillehammer, Norw. 17 F11
Lilongwe, Malawi 33 G6
Lima, Peru 40 F3
Limavady, U.K. 9 A5
Limerick, Ire. 9 D3
Límnos, Greece 15 E11
Limoges, France 12 C4
Limousin, □ France 12 C4
Limpopo, ≈ Africa 33 K6
Linares, Spain 13 C4
Lincoln, U.S.A. 37 B7
Lincoln, U.K. 6 D7
Lincolnshire, □ U.K. 6 D7
Linköping, Swed. 17 G13
Linz, Austria 10 D7
Lisboa, Port. 13 C1
Lisburn, U.K. 9 B5
Listowel, Ire. 9 D2
Lithuania, ■ Europe 18 D3
Little Minch, U.K. 8 D2
Little Rock, U.S.A. 37 D8
Liverpool, U.K. 6 D5
Livingston, U.K. 8 F5
Livingstone, Zambia 33 H5
Livorno, Italy 14 C4
Lizard, U.K. 7 H2
Ljubljana, Slovenia 14 A6
Llanelli, U.K. 7 F3
Lloret, Spain 13 B7
Lobito, Angola 33 G2
Locarno, L. di, Italy 14 A3
Lochaber, U.K. 8 E3
Lockerbie, U.K. 8 F5
Łódź, Poland 11 C9
Lofoten, Norw. 16 B12
Logroño, Spain 13 A4
Loire, ≈ France 12 C2
Lolland, Den. 17 J11
Lombardia, □ Italy 14 B3
Lombok, Indonesia 23 D3

Lomé, Togo 30 G5
Lomond, L., U.K. 8 E4
Łomza, Poland 11 B10
London, U.K. 7 F7
London, Canada 35 D11
Londonderry, U.K. 9 B4
Londrina, Brazil 42 A6
Long Beach, U.S.A. ...36 D3
Long Island, U.S.A. ...37 B12
Longford, □ Ire. 9 C4
Lorca, Spain 13 D5
Lorne, U.K. 8 E3
Lorraine, □ France 12 B7
Los Angeles, U.S.A. ..36 D3
Lothian, □ U.K. 8 F5
Loughborough, U.K. ...6 E6
Louisiana, □ U.S.A. ...37 D8
Louisville, U.S.A. 37 C9
Lourdes, France 12 E3
Louth, □ Ire. 9 C5
Lower Hutt, N.Z. 28 J5
Lowestoft, U.K. 7 E9
Luanda, Angola 32 F2
Luanshya, Zambia 33 G5
Lubbock, U.S.A. 36 D6
Lübeck, Ger. 10 B5
Lublin, Poland 11 C11
Lubumbashi, Zaïre 33 G5
Lucca, Italy 14 C4
Lucknow, India 22 C5
Ludwigshafen, Ger. ...10 D4
Lugo, Spain 13 A2
Lugansk, U.K. 9 B5
Lusaka, Zambia 33 H5
Luton, U.K. 7 F7
Luxembourg, ■ Europe ..10 D3
Luzern, Switz. 10 E4
Luzhou, China 25 D5
Luzon, Philippines ...23 B4
Lvov, Ukraine 18 E3
Lyckele, Swed. 16 D15
Lymington, U.K. 7 G6
Lyon, France 12 D6

M

M'Clintock Chan., Canada ..34 B9
Macapá, Brazil 41 C8
Macau, ■ Asia 25 D6
Macclesfield, U.K. 6 D5
Macdonnell Ranges, Australia ..26 C5
Macedonia = Makedhona,
□ Greece 15 D10
Maceió, Brazil 41 E11
Mackenzie, ≈ Canada ..34 B6
Mackenzie Mts., Canada ..34 B6
Macroom, Ire. 9 D2
Madagascar, ■ Africa ..33 J9
Madeira, Atl. Ocean ..30 B1
Madeira, ≈ S. Amer. ..40 E6
Madhya Pradesh, □ India ..22 D4
Madison, U.S.A. 37 B9
Madras, India 22 F5
Madre, L., Mexico ...38 B5
Madrid, □ Spain 13 B4
Madrid, Spain 13 B4
Madurai, India 22 G4
Maebashi, Japan 24 A6
Mafia I., Tanzania ...32 F7
Magadan, Russia 19 D16
Magalluf, Spain 13 C7
Magdeburg, Ger. 10 B5
Magherafelt, □ U.K. ..9 B5
Maharashtra, □ India ..22 D4
Mahon, Spain 13 C8
Mai-Ndombe, L., Zaïre ..32 E3
Maidenhead, U.K. 7 F7
Maidstone, U.K. 7 F8
Maiduguri, Nigeria ...31 F7
Maimana, Afghan. ...21 B5
Maine, □ France 12 B3
Maine, □ U.S.A. 37 A13
Mainz, Ger. 10 D4
Makasar = Ujung Pandang,
Indonesia 23 D3
Makedhona, □ Greece ..15 D10
Makedonija, □ Yug. ...15 D9
Makgadikgadi Salt Pans, Botswana ..33 J5
Makkah, S. Arabia ...21 C3
Malaga, Spain 13 D3
Malatya, Turkey 21 B2
Malawi, ■ Africa 33 G6
Malaysia, ■ Asia 23 C2
Maldives, ■ Ind. Ocean ..22 G3
Mali, ■ Africa 30 E4
Mallorca, Spain 13 C7
Mallow, Ire. 9 D3
Malmö, Swed. 17 J12
Malmöhus, □ Swed. ..17 J12
Malta, ■ Europe 14 G14
Malvern Hills, U.K. ...7 E5
Man, I. of, U.K. 6 C3
Managua, Nicaragua ..38 E7
Manaus, Brazil 40 D6
Manchester, U.K. 6 D5
Mandalay, Burma 22 D8

Manila, Philippines ...23 B4
Manitoba, □ Canada ..34 C10
Manitoba, L., Canada ..34 C10
Manizales, Colombia ..40 B3
Mannheim, Ger. 10 D4
Mansel I., Canada ...35 B11
Mansfield, U.K. 6 D6
Mantova, Italy 14 B4
Maputo, Mozambique ..33 K6
Mar del Plata, Argentina ..42 D5
Maracaibo, Venezuela ..40 A4
Maracay, Venezuela ..40 A5
Marajó, I. de, Brazil ..41 D9
Maranhão, □ Brazil ..41 E9
Marbella, Spain 13 D3
Marche, □ France ...12 C4
Marche, □ Italy 14 C5
Margate, U.K. 7 F9
Mariana Is., Pac. Ocean ..3 D17
Maribor, Slovenia ...14 A6
Marie-Galante, W. Indies ..38 M20
Marília, Brazil 41 H8
Maringá, Brazil 42 A6
Marmara, Sea of, Turkey ..21 A1
Marquesas Is., Pac. Ocean ..2 E3
Marrakech, Morocco ..30 B3
Marseille, France ...12 E6
Marshall Is., ■ Pac. Ocean ..3 D18
Martha's Vineyard, U.S.A. ..37 B12
Martinique, □ W. Indies ..38 N21
Maryland, □ U.S.A. ..37 C11
Mashhad, Iran 21 B4
Masqat, Oman 21 C4
Massachusetts, □ U.S.A. ..37 B12
Massif Central, France ..12 D5
Matadi, Zaïre 32 F2
Matamoros, Mexico ..38 B5
Mato Grosso, □ Brazil ..41 F7
Mato Grosso do Sul, □ Brazil ..41 G7
Matsuyama, Japan ...24 C3
Matterhorn, Switz. ..10 E3
Maturín, Venezuela ..40 B6
Mauritania, ■ Africa ..30 E2
Mauritius, ■ Ind. Ocean ..29 H9
Mayo, □ Ire. 9 C2
Mazar-i-Sharif, Afghan. ..21 B5
Mbandaka, Zaïre 32 D3
Meath, □ Ire. 9 C5
Mecca = Makkah, S. Arabia ..21 C2
Mechelen, Belgium ..10 C2
Medan, Indonesia ...23 C1
Medellín, Colombia ..40 B3
Medicine Hat, Canada ..34 D8
Medina = Al Madinah, S. Arabia ..21 C2
Mediterranean Sea, ..4 H7
Meerut, India 22 C4
Mekong, ≈ Asia 23 B2
Melbourne, Australia ..27 F8
Melrose, U.K. 8 F6
Melville I., Australia ..26 A5
Memphis, U.S.A. ...37 C9
Menai Strait, U.K. ..6 D3
Mendip Hills, U.K. ..7 F5
Mendoza, Argentina ..42 C3
Menorca, Spain 13 B7
Mentawai Is., Indonesia ..23 D1
Mérida, Mexico 38 C7
Mersey, ≈ U.K. 6 D5
Merseyside, □ U.K. ..6 D4
Merthyr Tydfil, U.K. ..7 F4
Messina, Italy 14 E6
Metz, France 12 B7
Mexicali, Mexico ...38 A1
Mexico, ■ Cent. Amer. ..38 B3
Mexico City, Mexico ..38 D5
Mexico, G. de, Cent. Amer. ..38 B6
Miami, U.S.A. 37 E10
Michigan, □ U.S.A. ..37 A9
Michigan, L., U.S.A. ..37 B9
Micronesia, ■ Pac. Ocean ..3 D17
Mid Glamorgan, □ U.K. ..7 F4
Middlesbrough, U.K. ..6 C6
Midland, U.S.A. 36 D6
Mikkeli, □ Fin. 16 E19
Milano, Italy 14 B3
Milton Keynes, U.K. ..7 E7
Milwaukee, U.S.A. ..37 B9
Minas Gerais, □ Brazil ..41 G9
Mindanao, Philippines ..23 C4
Minneapolis, U.S.A. ..37 B8
Minnesota, □ U.S.A. ..37 A8
Minsk, Belorussia ...18 D3
Miskolc, Hungary ...11 D10
Misrâtah, Libya 31 B8
Mississippi, □ U.S.A. ..37 D9
Mississippi, ≈ U.S.A. ..37 E9
Missouri, □ U.S.A. ..37 C8
Missouri, ≈ U.S.A. ..37 C8
Miyako, Japan 24 G11
Mobile, U.S.A. 37 D9
Mobutu, L., Africa ..32 D6
Moçambique, Mozambique ..33 H8
Módena, Italy 14 B4
Mogadishu, Somalia ..29 E8
Moldavia, ■ Europe ..18 E3
Moldova, □ Europe ..18 E3
Molise, □ Italy 14 C5
Mölndal, Swed. 17 H12
Moluccas, Indonesia ..23 C4

Mombasa, Kenya 32 E7
Mona, Canal de la, W. Indies ..39 D11
Monaco, ■ Europe ..12 E7
Monaghan, □ Ire. ..9 B5
Mönchengladbach, Ger. ..10 C3
Moncton, Canada ...35 D13
Mongolia, ■ Asia ...25 B5
Monrovia, Liberia ...30 G2
Mont St. - Michel, France ..12 B3
Montana, □ U.S.A. ..36 A4
Monte Carlo, Monaco ..12 E7
Montego Bay, Jamaica ..38 J16
Montenegro, □ Yug. ..15 C8
Monterrey, Mexico ..38 B4
Montes Claros, Brazil ..41 G10
Montevideo, Uruguay ..42 C5
Montgomery, U.S.A. ..37 D9
Montpellier, France ..12 E5
Montréal, Canada ...35 D12
Montrose, U.K. 8 E6
Montserrat, W. Indies ..38 L19
Moray Firth, U.K. ..8 D5
More og Romsdal, □ Norw. ..16 E9
Morecambe B., U.K. ..6 C4
Morelia, Mexico 38 D4
Morena, Sierra, Spain ..13 C3
Morioka, Japan 24 G11
Morocco, ■ Africa ..30 B3
Morvern, U.K. 8 E3
Moscow = Moskva, Russia ..18 D4
Mosel, ≈ Ger. 10 C3
Moskva, Russia 18 D4
Mostaganem, Algeria ..30 A5
Motala, Swed. 17 G13
Motherwell, U.K. ...8 F5
Moulamyaing, Burma ..22 E8
Mourne Mts., U.K. ..9 B5
Mozambique, ■ Africa ..33 J6
Mozambique Chan., Africa ..33 H8
Muck, U.K. 8 E2
Mufulira, Zambia ...33 G5
Mülheim, Ger. 10 C3
Mulhouse, France ..12 C7
Mull, U.K. 8 E3
Mullet Pen., Ire. ...9 B1
Mullingar, Ire. 9 C4
Multan, Pak. 22 B3
München, Ger. 10 D5
Munich = München, Ger. ..10 D5
Munster, Ire. 9 D3
Münster, Ger. 10 B3
Murcia, □ Spain ...13 C5
Murcia, Spain 13 C5
Murmansk, Russia ..18 C4
Muroran, Japan 24 F11
Murray River, ≈ Australia ..27 F6
Murray River Basin, Australia ..27 E7
Musgrave Ranges, Australia ..26 D5
Mustique, W. Indies ..38 Q20
Mwanza, Tanzania ..32 E6
Myanmar = Burma, ■ Asia ..22 D8
Mysore, India 22 F4

N

Nagano, Japan 24 A6
Nagaoka, Japan 24 G10
Nagasaki, Japan 24 C1
Nagoya, Japan 24 B5
Nagpur, India 22 D4
Nairobi, Kenya 32 E7
Nakhodka, Russia ...19 E14
Namaland, Namibia ..33 J3
Namibia, ■ Africa ..33 J3
Namibwoestyn, Namibia ..33 J2
Namsos, Norw. 16 D11
Nanchang, China ...25 D6
Nancy, France 12 B7
Nanjing, China 25 C6
Nanning, China 25 D5
Nansei-Shoto, Japan ..24 J8
Nantes, France 12 C3
Napier, N.Z. 28 H6
Napoli, Italy 14 D6
Narbonne, France ..12 E5
Narvik, Norw. 16 B14
Naser, Buheiret en, Egypt ..31 D11
Nashville, U.S.A. ...37 C9
Nassau, Bahamas ..39 B9
Natal, □ S. Africa ..33 K6
Natal, Brazil 41 E11
Nauru, ■ Pac. Ocean ..3 E18
Navarra, □ Spain ..13 A5
Náxos, Greece 15 F11
Ndjamena, Chad ...31 F8
Ndola, Zambia 33 G5
Nebraska, □ U.S.A. ..36 B6
Negro, ≈ Brazil ...40 D6
Neiva, Colombia ...40 C3
Nenagh, Ire. 9 D3
Nepal, ■ Asia 22 C5
Ness, L., U.K. 8 D4
Netherlands, ■ Europe ..10 B2
Nevada, □ U.S.A. ..36 C3
Nevers, France 12 C5
New Bedford, U.S.A. ..37 B12
New Britain, Pac. Ocean ..3 E17

New Brunswick, □ Canada ..35 D13
New Caledonia, Pac. Ocean ..3 F1
New Forest, U.K. ...7
New Hampshire, □ U.S.A. ..37 B1
New Haven, U.S.A. ..37 B1
New Jersey, □ U.S.A. ..37 B1
New Mexico, □ U.S.A. ..36 D
New Orleans, U.S.A. ..37 E
New Plymouth, N.Z. ..28
New Providence I., W. Indies ..39 B
New South Wales, □ Australia ..27 E
New York, U.S.A. ..37 B1
New York, □ U.S.A. ..37 B1
New Zealand, ■ Pac. Ocean ..28 J
Newark, U.S.A. 37 B1
Newbury, U.K. .....7 F
Newcastle, Australia ..27 E
Newcastle, U.K. ...6 C
Newcastle-under-Lyme, U.K. ..6 D
Newfoundland, □ Canada ..35 C
Newport, U.K. .....7 F
Newport News, U.S.A. ..37 C1
Newquay, U.K. ....7 G
Newry, U.K. ......9 B
Newtownabbey, □ U.K. ..9 B
Newtownards, □ U.K. ..9 B
Niagara Falls, N. Amer. ..35 D12
Niamey, Niger .....30 F
Nicaragua, ■ Cent. Amer. ..38 E
Nice, France ......12 E
Nicobar Is., India ..22 G1
Niederösterreich, □ Austria ..10 D
Niedersachsen, □ Ger. ..10 B
Niger, ■ Africa ....30 E
Niger, ≈ Africa ...30 G
Nigeria, ■ Africa ..30 G
Niigata, Japan 24 G10
Nijmegen, Neth. ...10 C2
Nîl el Abyad, ≈ Africa ..31 E1
Nîl el Azraq, ≈ Africa ..31 E1
Nîl, Nahr en, ≈ Africa ..31 C1
Nile = Nîl, Nahr en, ≈ Africa ..31 C11
Nîmes, France 12 E6
Ningbo, China 25 D7
Nishinomiya, Japan ..24 B4
Niteroi, Brazil 41 H10
Nizhniy Novgorod, Russia ..18 D5
Nord-Trondelag, □ Norw. ..16 E10
Nordland, □ Norw. ..16 C13
Nordrhein - Westfalen, □ Ger. ..10 C3
Norfolk, U.S.A. 37 C11
Norfolk, □ U.K. ...6 E8
Normandie, □ France ..12 B3
Norrbotten, □ Norw. ..16 C16
Norrköping, Swed. ..17 G14
North Carolina, □ U.S.A. ..37 C11
North Channel, Europe ..6 C4
North Dakota, □ U.S.A. ..36 A6
North Downs, U.K. ..7 F7
North Island, N.Z. ..28 G8
North Korea, ■ Asia ..25 B7
North Minch, U.K. ..8 C3
North Ronaldsay, U.K. ..8 B6
North Sea, Europe ..6 D8
North Uist, U.K. ...8 D1
North West Highlands, U.K. ..8 D3
North West Territories, □ Canada ..34 B8
North Yorkshire, □ U.K. ..6 C6
North Yorkshire Moors, U.K. ..6 C7
Northampton, U.K. ..7 E7
Northamptonshire, □ U.K. ..7 E7
Northern Ireland, □ U.K. ..9 B4
Northern Territory, □ Australia ..26 C5
Northumberland, □ U.K. ..6 B5
Norway, ■ Europe ..16 E11
Norwegian Sea, Atl. Ocean ..4 D6
Norwich, U.K. 6 E9
Nottingham, U.K. ..6 E6
Nottinghamshire, □ U.K. ..6 D6
Nouakchott, Mauritania ..30 E1
Nova Scotia, □ Canada ..35 D13
Novaya Zemlya, Russia ..18 B6
Novi Sad, Yug. 15 B8
Novokuznetsk, Russia ..18 D9
Novosibirsk, Russia ..18 D9
Novosibirskiye Ostrova, Russia ..19 B15
Nûbîya, Es Sahrâ en, Sudan ..31 D11
Nullarbor Plain, Australia ..26 E4
Nuneaton, U.K. ...7 E6
Nunivak I., Alaska ..34 B3
Nürnberg, Ger. 10 D5
Nyasa, L., Africa ..33 G6
Nykøbing, Den. 17 J12

O

Oakland, U.S.A. ...36 C2
Ob, ≈ Russia 18 C7
Oban, U.K. 8 E3
Oberhausen, Ger. ..10 C3
Oberösterreich, □ Austria ..10 D6
Obihiro, Japan 24 F11
Odense, Den. 17 J11
Oder, ≈ Europe ...10 B7
Odessa, Ukraine ...18 E4
Odessa, U.S.A. 36 D6
Offaly, □ Ire. 9 C4
Offenbach, Ger. ...10 C4
Ogbomosho, Nigeria ..30 G5

Ogden, U.S.A. ...36 B4
Ohio, ≈ U.S.A. ...37 C9
Ohio, □ U.S.A. ...37 B10
Okavango Swamps, Botswana ...33 H4
Okayama, Japan ...24 B3
Okazaki, Japan ...24 B5
Okhotsk, Russia ...19 D15
Okhotsk Sea of, Arctic ...19 D15
Oki-Shotō, Japan ...24 A3
Oklahoma, □ U.S.A. ...37 C7
Oklahoma City, U.S.A. ...37 C7
Okushiri-Tō, Japan ...24 F10
Oland, Swed. ...17 H14
Oldenburg, Ger. ...10 B4
Oldham, U.K. ...6 D6
Olimbos, Greece ...15 D10
Olomouc, Czech. ...10 D8
Olympia, Greece ...15 F9
Omagh, U.K. ...9 B4
Omaha, U.S.A. ...37 B7
Oman, ■ Asia ...21 C4
Oman, Gulf of, Asia ...21 C4
Omdurmân, Sudan ...31 E11
Omsk, Russia ...18 D8
Omuta, Japan ...24 C2
Onezhskoye, Ozero, Russia ...18 C4
Onitsha, Nigeria ...30 G6
Ontario, □ Canada ...35 C11
Ontario, L., N. Amer. ...35 D12
Opava, Czech. ...11 D8
Oppland, □ Norw. ...17 F10
Oradea, Rom. ...11 E10
Oran, Algeria ...30 A4
Oranje, ≈ S. Africa ...33 K3
Oranje-Vrystaat, □ S. Africa ...33 K5
Orebro, □ Swed. ...17 G13
Oregon, □ U.S.A. ...36 B2
Orense, Spain ...13 A2
Orinoco, ≈ S. Amer. ...40 B6
Orissa, □ India ...22 D5
Orkney, □ U.K. ...8 B5
Orlando, U.S.A. ...37 E10
Orleanais, □ France ...12 C4
Orleans, France ...12 C4
Orumiyeh, Iran ...21 B3
Oruro, Bolivia ...40 G5
Ōsaka, Japan ...24 B4
Oshawa, Canada ...35 D12
Oshogbo, Nigeria ...30 G5
Osijek, Croatia ...15 B8
Oskarshamn, Swed. ...17 H14
Oslo, Norw. ...17 G11
Osnabrück, Ger. ...10 B4
Östersund, Swed. ...16 E13
Ostfriesische Inseln, Ger. ...10 B3
Ostrava, Czech. ...11 D9
Ostrov Vrangelya, Russia ...19 B18
Ōsumi-Kaikyō, Japan ...24 D2
Ōsumi-Shotō, Japan ...24 D2
Otaru, Japan ...24 F11
Otranto, Str. of, Italy ...15 D8
Ottawa, Canada ...35 D12
Ötztal, Austria ...10 E5
Ouagadougou, Burkina Faso ...30 F4
Oujda, Morocco ...30 B4
Oulu, Fin. ...16 D18
Outer Hebrides, U.K. ...8 D1
Oviedo, Spain ...13 A3
Owambo, Namibia ...33 H3
Ox Mts., Ire. ...9 B3
Oxford, U.K. ...7 F6
Oxfordshire, □ U.K. ...7 F6

P

Pacaraima, Sierra, S. Amer. ...40 C6
Pacific Ocean, ...2 D3
Padang, Indonesia ...23 D2
Pádova, Italy ...14 B4
Paisley, U.K. ...8 F4
Pakistan, ■ Asia ...22 C2
Palawan, Philippines ...23 B3
Palembang, Indonesia ...23 D2
Palencia, Spain ...13 A3
Palermo, Italy ...14 E5
Palma, Spain ...13 C7
Palmerston North, N.Z. ...28 J5
Palmira, Colombia ...40 C3
Pamplona, Spain ...13 A5
Panama, ■ Cent. Amer. ...39 F8
Panama Canal, Panama ...38 H14
Panama City, Panama ...39 H14
Panama, G. de, Panama ...39 H14
Papua New Guinea, ■ Pac. Ocean ...3 E17
Pará, □ Brazil ...41 D8
Paraguay, ■ S. Amer. ...42 A5
Paraíba, □ Brazil ...41 E11
Parana, ≈ S. Amer. ...42 C5
Paraná, □ Brazil ...42 A6
Paraná, Argentina ...42 C4
Parecis, Serra dos, Brazil ...40 F6
Paris, France ...12 B5
Parma, Italy ...14 B4
Pasadena, U.S.A. ...36 D3
Pasto, Colombia ...40 C3
Patna, India ...22 C6
Patos L. dos, Brazil ...42 C6
Patrai, Greece ...15 E9

Pavia, Italy ...14 B3
Pecs, Hungary ...11 E9
Peking = Beijing, China ...25 C6
Peloponnisos, □ Greece ...15 F10
Pelotas, Brazil ...42 C6
Pemba I., Tanzania ...32 F7
Pennine Range, U.K. ...6 C5
Pennsylvania, □ U.S.A. ...37 B11
Pentland Firth, U.K. ...8 C5
Penzance, U.K. ...7 G2
Peoria, U.S.A. ...37 B9
Pereira, Colombia ...40 C3
Perm, Russia ...18 D6
Pernambuco, □ Brazil ...41 E11
Perpignan, France ...12 E5
Perth, Australia ...26 E2
Perth, U.K. ...8 E5
Peru, ■ S. Amer. ...40 E3
Perúgia, Italy ...14 C5
Pésaro, Italy ...14 C5
Pescara, Italy ...14 C6
Peshawar, Pak. ...22 B3
Peterboro', Canada ...35 D12
Peterborough, U.K. ...7 E7
Peterhead, U.K. ...8 D7
Petropavlovsk-Kamchatskiy, Russia ...19 D16
Petrópolis, Brazil ...41 H10
Pforzheim, Ger. ...10 D4
Phanh Bho Ho Chi Minh, Vietnam ...23 B2
Philadelphia, U.S.A. ...37 B12
Philippi, Greece ...15 D11
Philippines, ■ Asia ...23 B4
Phnom Penh, Cambodia ...23 B2
Phoenix, U.S.A. ...36 D4
Phoenix Is., Pac. Ocean ...2 E1
Piacenza, Italy ...14 B3
Piaui, □ Brazil ...41 E10
Picardie, □ France ...12 A5
Piemonte, □ Italy ...14 B2
Pietermaritzburg, S. Africa ...33 K6
Pindos Oros, Greece ...15 E9
Piotrków Trybunalsk, Poland ...11 C9
Piracicaba, Brazil ...41 H9
Piraievs, Greece ...15 F10
Pisa, Italy ...14 C4
Pistóia, Italy ...14 C4
Piteå, Swed. ...16 D16
Pittsburgh, U.S.A. ...37 B11
Plauen, Ger. ...10 C6
Pleven, Bulg. ...15 C11
Ploieşti, Rom. ...11 F13
Plovdiv, Bulg. ...15 C11
Plymouth, U.K. ...7 G3
Plzeň, Czech. ...10 D6
Po, ≈ Italy ...14 B5
Pointe Noire, Congo ...32 E2
Pointe-à Pitre, Guadeloupe ...38 L20
Poitou, □ France ...12 C3
Poland, ■ Europe ...11 C9
Ponce, Puerto Rico ...39 D11
Pondicherry, India ...22 F4
Ponta Grossa, Brazil ...42 B6
Pontefract, U.K. ...6 D6
Pontevedra, Spain ...13 A1
Pontiac, U.S.A. ...37 B10
Pontypool, U.K. ...7 F4
Pontypridd, U.K. ...7 F4
Poole, U.K. ...7 G6
Poona = Pune, India ...22 E3
Poopó, L., Bolivia ...40 G5
Popocatepetl, Mexico ...38 D5
Pori, Fin. ...17 F16
Port au Prince, Haiti ...39 D10
Port Elizabeth, S. Africa ...33 L5
Port Glasgow, U.K. ...8 F4
Port Harcourt, Nigeria ...30 H6
Port Laoise, Ire. ...9 C4
Port of Spain, Trinidad ...38 S20
Port Said = Bûr Saîd, Egypt ...31 B11
Port Talbot, U.K. ...7 F4
Portland, U.S.A. ...36 A2
Porto, Port. ...13 B1
Pôrto Alegre, Brazil ...42 C6
Portree, U.K. ...8 D2
Portsmouth, U.K. ...7 G6
Portsmouth, U.S.A. ...37 C11
Portugal, ■ Europe ...13 C1
Potosí, Bolivia ...40 G5
Potsdam, Ger. ...10 B6
Powys, □ U.K. ...7 E4
Poznan, Poland ...11 B8
Prague = Praha, Czech. ...10 C7
Praha, Czech. ...10 C7
Prato, Italy ...14 C4
Preston, U.K. ...6 D5
Pretoria, S. Africa ...33 K5
Prince Albert, Canada ...34 C9
Prince Charles I., Canada ...35 B12
Prince Edward I., □ Canada ...35 D13
Prince of Wales I., Alaska ...34 C6
Prince of Wales I., Canada ...34 A10
Provence, □ France ...12 E6
Providence, U.S.A. ...37 B12
Puebla, Mexico ...38 D5
Pueblo, U.S.A. ...36 C6
Puerto Rico, ■ W. Indies ...39 D11
Puglia, □ Italy ...14 D7
Pula, Croatia ...14 B5
Pune, India 22 E3

Punjab, □ India ...22 B4
Purbeck, I. of, U.K. ...7 G5
Pusan, S. Korea ...25 C7
Pyongyang, N. Korea ...25 C7
Pyrénées, France ...12 E4

Q

Qatar, ■ Asia ...21 C4
Qingdao, China ...25 C7
Qiqihar, China ...25 B7
Quantock Hills, U.K. ...7 F4
Quebec, □ Canada ...35 C13
Quebec, Canada ...35 D12
Queen Charlotte Is., Canada ...34 C6
Queen Maud Gulf, Canada ...34 B9
Queensland, □ Australia ...27 C7
Quezon City, Philippines ...23 B4
Quito, Ecuador ...40 D3

R

Rabat, Morocco ...30 B3
Radom, Poland ...11 C10
Ragusa, Italy ...14 F6
Rajasthan, □ India ...22 C3
Ramsgate, U.K. ...7 F9
Randers, Den. ...17 H11
Rangoon, Burma ...22 E8
Rasht, Iran ...21 B3
Rauma, Fin. ...17 F16
Rawalpindi, Pak. ...22 B3
Reading, U.K. ...7 F7
Rebun-Tō, Japan ...24 E11
Recife, Brazil ...41 E12
Red River, ≈ U.S.A. ...37 D8
Red Sea, Asia ...21 C2
Redditch, U.K. ...7 E6
Regensburg, Ger. ...10 D6
Réggio di Calábria, Italy ...14 E6
Réggio nell'Emilia, Italy ...14 B4
Regina, Canada ...34 C9
Reichenbach, Ger. ...10 C6
Reigate, U.K. ...7 F7
Reims, France ...12 B6
Reina Adelaida, Arch., Chile ...42 G2
Reindeer L., Canada ...34 C9
Remscheid, Ger. ...10 C3
Rennes, France ...12 B3
Reno, U.S.A. ...36 C3
Réunion, ■ Ind. Ocean ...29 H9
Reykjavik, Iceland ...16 D3
Rhein, ≈ Europe ...10 C3
Rheinland Pfalz, □ Ger. ...10 D3
Rhine = Rhein, ≈ Ger. ...10 C3
Rhode Island, □ U.S.A. ...37 B12
Rhodes = Ródhos, Greece ...15 F13
Rhodopi Planina, Bulg. ...15 D11
Rhön, Ger. ...10 C5
Rhondda, U.K. ...7 F4
Rhône, ≈ France ...12 D6
Ribeirão Prêto, Brazil ...41 H9
Richmond, U.K. ...7 F7
Richmond, U.S.A. ...37 C11
Riga, Latvia ...18 D3
Rijeka, Croatia ...14 B6
Rimini, Italy ...14 B5
Rio Branco, Brazil ...40 E5
Rio de Janeiro, Brazil ...41 H10
Rio Gallegos, Argentina ...42 G3
Rio Grande, Brazil ...42 C6
Rio Grande do Norte, □ Brazil ...41 E11
Rio Grande do Sul, □ Brazil ...42 B6
Rishiri-Tō, Japan ...24 E11
Riyadh = Ar Riyād, S. Arabia ...21 C3
Rochefort, France ...12 D3
Rochester, U.K. ...7 F8
Rochester, U.S.A. ...37 B11
Rocky Mts., N. Amer. ...36 A4
Ródhos, Greece ...15 F13
Rogaland, □ Norw. ...17 G9
Roma, Italy ...14 D5
Romania, ■ Europe ...11 F12
Rondônia, □ Brazil ...40 F6
Roodepoort-Maraisburg, S. Africa ...33 K5
Roraima, □ Brazil ...40 C6
Rosario, Argentina ...42 C4
Roscommon, □ Ire. ...9 C3
Roseau, Dominica ...38 M20
Roskilde, Den. ...17 J12
Rostock, Ger. ...10 A6
Rostov, Russia ...18 E4
Rotherham, U.K. ...6 D6
Rotterdam, Neth. ...10 C2
Roubaix, Belgium ...10 C1
Rouen, France ...12 B4
Rousay, U.K. ...8 B5
Ruse, Bulg. ...11 D13
Russian Federation, ■ Europe/Asia ...18 C7
Rwanda, ■ Africa ...32 E5
Ryde, U.K. ...7 G6

S

's-Gravenhage, Neth. ...10 B2
's-Hertogenbosch, Neth. ...10 C2

Saarbrucken, Ger. ...10 D3
Saarland, □ Ger. ...10 D3
Sabadell, Spain ...13 B6
Sabah, □ Malaysia ...23 C3
Sacramento, U.S.A. ...36 C2
Sado, Japan ...24 G10
Safi, Morocco ...30 B3
Saginaw, U.S.A. ...37 B10
Sahara, Africa ...30 D4
Saigon = Phanh Bho Ho Chi Minh, Vietnam ...23 B2
Saint John, Canada ...35 D13
Saintonge, □ France ...12 D3
Sakai, Japan ...24 B4
Sakata, Japan ...24 G10
Sakhalin, Russia ...19 D15
Salamanca, Spain ...13 B3
Salerno, Italy ...14 D6
Salford, U.K. ...6 D5
Salisbury, U.K. ...7 F6
Salt Lake City, U.S.A. ...36 B4
Salta, Argentina ...42 A3
Saltillo, Mexico ...38 B4
Salvador, Brazil ...41 F11
Salzburg, Austria ...10 E6
Salzgitter, Ger. ...10 B5
Samara, Russia ...18 D6
Samarkand, Uzbekistan ...18 F7
Samoan Is., Pac. Ocean ...28 A12
Sámos, Greece ...15 F12
Samothráki, Greece ...15 D11
San Angelo, U.S.A. ...36 D6
San Antonio, U.S.A. ...36 E7
San Cristóbal, Venezuela ...40 B4
San Diego, U.S.A. ...36 D3
San Fernando, Trinidad ...38 S20
San Francisco, U.S.A. ...36 C2
San Francisco de Macoris, Dom. Rep. ...39 D10
San Jose, U.S.A. ...36 C2
San Juan, Argentina ...42 C3
San Juan, Puerto Rico ...39 D11
San Luis Potosi, Mexico ...38 C4
San Marino, ■ Europe ...14 C5
San Miguel de Tucuman, Argentina ...42 B3
San Salvador, El Salvador ...38 E7
San Sebastian, Spain ...13 A4
San'a, Yemen ...21 D3
Sancti Spiritus, Cuba ...39 C9
Sanday, U.K. ...8 B6
Santa Ana, U.S.A. ...36 D3
Santa Barbara, U.S.A. ...36 D3
Santa Catarina, □ Brazil ...42 B7
Santa Clara, Cuba ...39 C9
Santa Clara, U.S.A. ...36 C2
Santa Cruz, Bolivia ...40 G6
Santa Cruz, Canary Is. ...30 C1
Santa Fe, Argentina ...42 C4
Santa Marta, Colombia ...40 A4
Santander, Spain ...13 A4
Santarém, Brazil ...41 D8
Santarém, Port. ...13 C1
Santiago, Chile ...42 C2
Santiago, Dom. Rep. ...39 D10
Santiago, Spain ...13 A1
Santiago de Cuba, Cuba ...39 C9
Santo Domingo, Dom. Rep. ...39 D11
Santos, Brazil ...42 A7
São Francisco, ≈ Brazil ...41 F11
São Luís, Brazil ...41 D10
São Paulo, □ Brazil ...41 H9
São Paulo, Brazil ...42 A7
São Tomé & Principe, ■ Africa ...29 E4
Sapporo, Japan ...24 F11
Sarajevo, Yug. ...15 C8
Saratov, Russia ...18 D5
Sarawak, □ Malaysia ...23 C3
Sardegna, □ Italy ...14 D3
Sardinia = Sardegna, □ Italy ...14 D3
Sark, Channel Is. ...12 B2
Sasebo, Japan ...24 C1
Saskatchewan, □ Canada ...34 C9
Saskatoon, Canada ...34 C9
Satu Mare, Rom. ...11 E11
Saudi Arabia, ■ Asia ...21 C3
Sault Ste. Marie, Canada ...35 D11
Savannah, U.S.A. ...37 D10
Savoie, □ France ...12 D7
Savona, Italy ...14 B3
Scapa Flow, U.K. ...8 C5
Scarborough, U.K. ...6 C7
Schleswig-Holstein, □ Ger. ...10 A4
Schwäbische Alb, Ger. ...10 D4
Schwarzwald, Ger. ...10 D4
Schwerin, Ger. ...10 B5
Scilly, Is. of, U.K. ...7 H2
Scotland, □ U.K. ...8 E4
Scunthorpe, U.K. ...6 D6
Seattle, U.S.A. ...36 A2
Segovia, Spain ...13 B3
Seine, ≈ France ...12 B5
Sekondi - Takoradi, Ghana ...30 H4
Selkirk, U.K. ...8 F6
Semarang, Indonesia ...23 D3
Sendai, Japan ...24 G11
Senegal, ■ Africa ...30 F2
Sŏul, S. Korea ...25 C7
Serbia, □ Yug. ...15 C9
Setonaikai, Japan ...24 C3

Setúbal, Port. ...13 C1
Sevastopol, Ukraine ...18 E4
Severn, ≈ U.K. ...7 F5
Severnaya Zemlya, Russia ...19 B10
Sevilla, Spain ...13 D3
Seychelles, ■ Ind. Ocean ...3 E12
Sfax, Tunisia ...31 B7
Shache, China ...25 C2
Shanghai, China ...25 C7
Shannon, ≈ Ire. ...9 D2
Shantou, China ...25 D6
Shapinsay, U.K. ...8 B6
Sheffield, U.K. ...6 D6
Shenyang, China ...25 B7
Sherwood Forest, U.K. ...6 D6
Shetland, □ U.K. ...8 A7
Shikoku, Japan ...24 C3
Shimonoseki, Japan ...24 C2
Shirāz, Iran ...21 C4
Shizuoka, Japan ...24 B6
Sholapur, India ...22 E4
Shreveport, U.S.A. ...37 D8
Shrewsbury, U.K. ...6 E5
Shropshire, □ U.K. ...7 E5
Siam = Thailand, ■ Asia ...23 B2
Sibiu, Rom. ...11 F12
Sichuan, □ China ...25 D5
Sicilia, □ Italy ...14 F5
Siena, Italy ...14 C4
Sierra Leone, ■ Africa ...30 G2
Sierra Nevada, U.S.A. ...36 C3
Silver City, Panama ...38 H14
Simpson Desert, Australia ...26 C6
Singapore, ■ Asia ...23 C2
Sioux City, U.S.A. ...37 B7
Sioux Falls, U.S.A. ...37 B7
Siracusa, Italy ...14 F6
Sitges, Spain ...13 B6
Sjælland, Den. ...17 J11
Skagerrak, Europe ...17 H10
Skien, Norw. ...17 G10
Skikda, Algeria ...30 A6
Skopje, Yug. ...15 C9
Skye, I. of, U.K. ...8 D2
Slieve Aughty, Ire. ...9 C3
Slieve Bloom, Ire. ...9 C4
Slieve Mish, Ire. ...9 D2
Sligo, Ire. ...9 B3
Slough, U.K. ...7 F7
Slovak Rep., ■ Czech. ...11 D9
Slovenia, ■ Europe ...14 B6
Snake, ≈ U.S.A. ...36 A3
Snowdon, U.K. ...6 D3
Society Is., Pac. Ocean ...2 E2
Socotra, Yemen ...21 D4
Söderhamn, Swed. ...17 F14
Sofiya, Bulg. ...15 C10
Sogn og Fjordane, □ Norw. ...17 F9
Solimoes, ≈ Brazil ...40 D5
Solomon Is., ■ Pac. Ocean ...3 E17
Solway Firth, U.K. ...6 C5
Somali Rep., ■ Africa ...29 E8
Somerset, □ U.K. ...7 F4
Somerset I., Canada ...34 A10
Sŏr-Trondelag, □ Norw. ...16 D12
Soria, Spain ...13 B4
Sorocaba, Brazil ...42 A7
Sosnowiec, Poland ...11 C9
Sousse, Tunisia ...31 A7
South Africa, ■ Africa ...33 L3
South Australia, □ Australia ...26 D5
South Bend, U.S.A. ...37 B9
South Carolina, □ U.S.A. ...37 D10
South China Sea, Asia ...23 B3
South Dakota, □ U.S.A. ...36 B6
South Downs, U.K. ...7 G7
South Georgia, Atl. Ocean ...42 G9
South Glamorgan, □ U.K. ...7 F4
South Island, N.Z. ...28 K3
South Korea, ■ Asia ...25 C7
South Ronaldsay, U.K. ...8 C6
South Shields, U.K. ...6 C6
South Uist, U.K. ...8 D1
South Yorkshire, □ U.K. ...6 D6
Southampton, U.K. ...7 G6
Southampton I., Canada ...35 B11
Southend, U.K. ...7 F8
Southern Alps, N.Z. ...28 K3
Southern Ocean, ...3 G12
Southern Uplands, U.K. ...8 F5
Southport, U.K. ...6 D4
Soutpansberg, S. Africa ...33 J5
Spain, ■ Europe ...13 B4
Spandau, Ger. ...10 B6
Spanish Town, Jamaica ...38 K17
Spencer Gulf, Australia ...27 E6
Sperrin Mts., U.K. ...9 B4
Spessart, Ger. ...10 D4
Split, Croatia ...14 C7
Spokane, U.S.A. ...36 A3
Sporádhes Voríai, Greece ...15 E11
Springfield, U.S.A. ...37 B12
Springs, S. Africa ...33 K5
Sri Lanka, ■ Asia ...22 G5
Srinagar, India ...22 B3
St. Albans, U.K. ...7 F7
St. Andrews, U.K. ...8 E6
St. Austell, U.K. ...7 G3
St. Boniface, Canada ...34 D10

Index

St. Croix, *W. Indies* 39 D12
St. - Étienne, *France* 12 D6
St. Gallen, *Switz.* 10 E4
St. George's, *Grenada* 38 Q20
St. George's Channel, *Europe* ...9 E5
St. Helena, *Atl. Ocean* 29 G3
St. Helens, *U.K.* 6 D5
St. John's, *Antigua* 38 K20
St. John's, *Canada* 35 D14
St. Kitts - Nevis, ■ *W. Indies* ...38 K19
St. Lawrence, ≈ *Canada* 35 D14
St. Louis, *U.S.A.* 37 C8
St. Lucia, ■ *W. Indies* 38 P21
St. Maarten, □ *W. Indies* 38 J18
St. Malo, *France* 12 B2
St. Martin, □ *W. Indies* 38 J18
St. Michael's Mt., *U.K.* 7 G2
St. Nazaire, *France* 12 C2
St. Paul, *U.S.A.* 37 B8
St. Peterburg, *Russia* 18 D4
St. Petersburg, *U.S.A.* 37 E10
St. Pierre et Miquelon, □ *N. Amer.* .35 D14
St. Thomas, *W. Indies* 39 D12
St. - Denis, *France* 12 B5
St. - Tropez, *France* 12 E7
St. Vincent & the Grenadines,
  ■ *W. Indies* 38 P20
Stafford, *U.K.* 6 E5
Staffordshire, □ *U.K.* 6 E5
Staines, *U.K.* 7 F7
Stalingrad = Volgograd, *Russia* ..18 E5
Stanley, *Falkland Is.* 42 G5
Stara Planina, *Bulg.* 15 C11
Stavanger, *Norw.* 17 G8
Steiermark, □ *Austria* 10 E7
Sterea Ellas, □ *Greece* 15 E9
Stewart I., *N.Z.* 28 M1
Stirling, *U.K.* 8 E5
Stockholm, *Swed.* 17 G15
Stockport, *U.K.* 6 D5
Stockton, *U.K.* 6 C6
Stockton, *U.S.A.* 36 C2
Stoke-on-Trent, *U.K.* 6 D5
Stonehenge, *U.K.* 7 F6
Stourbridge, *U.K.* 7 E5
Strabane, *U.K.* 9 B4
Stralsund, *Ger.* 10 A6
Strasbourg, *France* 12 B7
Stratford-on-Avon, *U.K.* 7 E6
Strath Spey, *U.K.* 8 D5
Strathclyde, □ *U.K.* 8 F3
Stromeferry, *U.K.* 8 D3
Stronsay, *U.K.* 8 B6
Stuttgart, *Ger.* 10 D4
Subotica, *Yug.* 15 A8
Sucre, *Bolivia* 40 G5
Sudan, ■ *Africa* 31 E10
Sudbury, *Canada* 35 D11
Suez Canal, *Egypt* 21 B2
Suez = El Suweis, *Egypt* 31 C11
Suffolk, □ *U.K.* 7 E8
Sulawesi, *Indonesia* 23 D4
Sumatera, *Indonesia* 23 D2
Sumba, *Indonesia* 23 D4
Sumbawa, *Indonesia* 23 D3
Sunderland, *U.K.* 6 C6
Sundsvall, *Swed.* 16 E14
Superior, L., *N. Amer.* 37 A9
Surabaja, *Indonesia* 23 D3
Surat, *India* 22 D3
Surinam, ■ *S. Amer.* 41 C7
Surrey, □ *U.K.* 7 F7
Sutton-in-Ashfield, *U.K.* 6 D6
Suva, *Fiji* 28 D8
Suzhou, *China* 25 C7
Svendborg, *Den.* 17 J11
Sverdlovsk = Yekaterinburg, *Russia* 18 D7
Swansea, *U.K.* 7 F4
Swaziland, ■ *Africa* 33 K6
Sweden, ■ *Europe* 17 F13
Swindon, *U.K.* 7 F6
Switzerland, ■ *Europe* 10 E3
Sydney, *Australia* 27 E9
Syracuse, *U.S.A.* 37 B11
Syria, ■ *Asia* 21 B2
Syrian Desert, *Asia* 21 B2
Szczecin, *Poland* 10 B7
Szeged, *Hungary* 11 E10

T

Tabrīz, *Iran* 21 B3
Tacoma, *U.S.A.* 36 A2
Taegu, *S. Korea* 25 C7
Tahiti, *Pac. Ocean* 2 E2
Taibei, *Taiwan* 25 D7
Tainan, *Taiwan* 25 D7
Taiwan, ■ *Asia* 25 D7
Taiyuan, *China* 25 C6
Taizhong, *Taiwan* 25 D7
Tajikistan, ■ *Asia* 18 F7
Takamatsu, *Japan* 24 B4
Talcahuano, *Chile* 42 D2
Tallinn, *Estonia* 18 D3
Tamil Nadu, □ *India* 22 F4
Tampa, *U.S.A.* 37 E10
Tampere, *Fin.* 17 F17
Tampico, *Mexico* 38 C5
Tamworth, *U.K.* 7 E6

Tane-ga-Shima, *Japan* 24 D2
Tanga, *Tanzania* 32 F7
Tanganyika, L., *Africa* 32 F5
Tanger, *Morocco* 30 A3
Tangshan, *China* 25 C6
Tanimbar Is., *Indonesia* 23 D5
Tanta, *Egypt* 31 B11
Tanzania, ■ *Africa* 32 F7
Tarābulus, *Lebanon* 21 B2
Tarābulus, *Libya* 31 B7
Taranto, *Italy* 14 D7
Tarragona, *Spain* 13 B6
Tarrasa, *Spain* 13 B6
Tashkent, *Uzbekistan* 18 E7
Tasman Sea, *Pac. Ocean* 28 A2
Tasmania, *Australia* 27 G8
Tauern, *Austria* 10 E6
Taunton, *U.K.* 7 F4
Taunus, *Ger.* 10 C4
Tay, ≈ *U.K.* 8 E5
Tayside, □ *U.K.* 8 E5
Tbilisi, *Georgia* 18 E5
Tchad, L., *Chad* 31 F7
Teeside, *U.K.* 6 C6
Tegucigalpa, *Honduras* 38 E7
Tehrān, *Iran* 21 B4
Tehuantepec, Istme de, *Mexico* .38 D5
Tejo, ≈ *Port.* 13 C1
Tel Aviv - Yafo, *Israel* 21 B2
Telemark, □ *Norw.* 17 G10
Telford, *U.K.* 6 E5
Tenerife, *Canary Is.* 30 C1
Tennessee, □ *U.S.A.* 37 C9
Tennessee, ≈ *U.S.A.* 37 C9
Teresina, *Brazil* 41 E10
Terni, *Italy* 14 C5
Teruel, *Spain* 13 B5
Tetouan, *Morocco* 30 A3
Teutoburger Wald, *Ger.* 10 B4
Tevere, ≈ *Italy* 14 C5
Texas, □ *U.S.A.* 36 D6
Thailand, ■ *Asia* 23 B2
Thames, ≈ *U.K.* 7 F8
Thásos, *Greece* 15 D11
The Hague = 's-Gravenhage, *Neth.* .10 B2
Thessalia, □ *Greece* 15 E10
Thessaloníka, *Greece* 15 D10
Thies, *Senegal* 30 F1
Thráki, □ *Greece* 15 D11
Thunder Bay, *Canada* 35 D11
Thüringer Wald, *Ger.* 10 C5
Thurles, *Ire.* 9 D4
Thurso, *U.K.* 8 C5
Tianjin, *China* 25 C6
Tiber = Tevere, ≈ *Italy* 14 C5
Tibesti, *Chad* 31 D8
Tibet = Xizang, □ *China* 25 C3
Tientsin = Tianjin, *China* 25 C6
Tierra del Fuego, *S. Amer.* 42 G3
Tigris, ≈ *Iraq* 21 B3
Tijuana, *Mexico* 38 A1
Tilburg, *Neth.* 10 C2
Timaru, *N.Z.* 28 L3
Timişoara, *Rom.* 11 F10
Timor, *Indonesia* 23 D4
Tínos, *Greece* 15 F11
Tipperary, □ *Ire.* 9 D4
Tipperary, *Ire.* 9 D3
Tipton, *U.K.* 7 E5
Tiranë, *Alb.* 15 D8
Tirol, □ *Austria* 10 E5
Tiruchchirappalli, *India* 22 F4
Titicaca, L., *S. Amer.* 40 G5
Titograd, *Yug.* 15 C8
Tizi-Ouzou, *Algeria* 30 A5
Tobago, *W. Indies* 39 E12
Togo, ■ *Africa* 30 G5
Tokelau Is., *Pac. Ocean* 2 E1
Tōkyo, *Japan* 24 B6
Toledo, *Spain* 13 C3
Toledo, *U.S.A.* 37 B10
Toluca, *Mexico* 38 D5
Tomsk, *Russia* 18 D9
Tonga, ■ *Pac. Ocean* 28 D11
Toowoomba, *Australia* 27 D9
Topeka, *U.S.A.* 37 C7
Torbay, *U.K.* 7 G4
Torino, *Italy* 14 B2
Toronto, *Canada* 35 D12
Torquay, *U.K.* 7 G4
Torremolinos, *Spain* 13 D3
Torrens, L., *Australia* 27 E6
Torreón, *Mexico* 38 B4
Tortosa, *Spain* 13 B6
Toruń, *Poland* 11 B9
Toscana, □ *Italy* 14 C4
Toulon, *France* 12 E6
Toulouse, *France* 12 E4
Touraine, □ *France* 12 C4
Tourcoing, *Belgium* 10 C1
Tours, *France* 12 C4
Townsville, *Australia* 27 B8
Toyama, *Japan* 24 A5
Toyohashi, *Japan* 24 B5
Toyonaka, *Japan* 24 B4
Tralee, *Ire.* 9 D2
Transilvania, *Rom.* 11 E12
Transvaal, □ *S. Africa* 33 K5

Trápani, *Italy* 14 E5
Trelleborg, *Swed.* 17 J12
Trentino Alto-Adige, □ *Italy* 14 A4
Treviso, *Italy* 14 B5
Trier, *Ger.* 10 D3
Trieste, *Italy* 14 B5
Trincomalee, *Sri Lanka* 22 G5
Trinidad & Tobago, ■ *W. Indies* .39 E12
Tripoli = Tarābulus, *Libya* 31 B7
Tristan da Cunha, *Atl. Ocean* 2 F9
Trois-Rivières, *Canada* 35 D12
Trollhätten, *Swed.* 17 G12
Troms, □ *Norw.* 16 B15
Tromsø, *Norw.* 16 B15
Trondheim, *Norw.* 16 E11
Trossachs, *U.K.* 8 E4
Trujillo, *Peru* 40 E3
Tsugaru-Kaikyō, *Japan* 24 F11
Tsushima, *Japan* 24 H8
Tuamotu Arch., *Pac. Ocean* 2 E3
Tubuai Is., *Pac. Ocean* 2 F2
Tucson, *U.S.A.* 36 D4
Tula, *Russia* 18 D4
Tullamore, *Ire.* 9 C4
Tulsa, *U.S.A.* 37 C7
Tulua, *Colombia* 40 C3
Tunis, *Tunisia* 30 A6
Tunisia, ■ *Africa* 30 A6
Turin = Torino, *Italy* 14 B2
Turkana, L., *Kenya* 32 D7
Turkey, ■ *Asia* 21 B2
Turkmenistan, ■ *Asia* 18 F6
Turku, *Fin.* 17 F17
Turnu-Severin, *Rom.* 11 F11
Turun ja Pori, *Fin.* 17 F17
Tuvalu, ■ *Pac. Ocean* 3 E18
Tver, *Russia* 18 D4
Tyler, *U.S.A.* 37 D7
Tyne & Wear, □ *U.K.* 6 C6
Tynemouth, *U.K.* 6 C6
Tyrrhenian Sea, *Italy* 14 E5

U

Uberaba, *Brazil* 41 G9
Uddevalla, *Swed.* 17 G11
Udine, *Italy* 14 A5
Ufa, *Russia* 18 D6
Uganda, ■ *Africa* 32 D6
Újpest, *Hungary* 11 E9
Ujung Pandang, *Indonesia* 23 D3
Ukraine, ■ *Europe* 18 E4
Ulaanbaatar, *Mong.* 25 B5
Ulan Ude, *Russia* 19 D11
Ullapool, *U.K.* 8 D3
Ulm, *Ger.* 10 D4
Ulster, *U.K.* 9 B4
Umbria, □ *Italy* 14 C5
Ungava Pen., *Canada* 35 C12
United Arab Emirates, ■ *Asia* 21 C4
United Kingdom, ■ *Europe* 4 E5
United States of America, ■
  N. Amer. 36 C6
Unst, *U.K.* 8 A8
Uppsala, *Swed.* 17 G14
Urmia, L., *Iran* 21 B3
Uruguay, ■ *S. Amer.* 42 C5
Uruguay, ≈ *S. Amer.* 42 C5
Urumqi, *China* 25 B3
Usti nad Labem, *Czech.* 10 C7
Utah, □ *U.S.A.* 36 C4
Utrecht, *Neth.* 10 B2
Utsunomiya, *Japan* 24 A6
Uttar Pradesh, □ *India* 22 C5
Uudenmaa, □ *Fin.* 17 F18
Uzbekistan, ■ *Asia* 18 E7

V

Vaal, ≈ *S. Africa* 33 K4
Vaasa, □ *Fin.* 16 E17
Vadso, *Norw.* 16 A20
Valence, *France* 12 D6
Valencia, □ *Spain* 13 C5
Valencia, *Spain* 13 C5
Valencia, *Venezuela* 40 A5
Valladolid, *Spain* 13 B3
Valle d'Aosta, *Italy* 14 B2
Valletta, *Malta* 14 G15
Valparaíso, *Chile* 42 C2
Vancouver, *Canada* 34 D7
Vancouver I., *Canada* 34 D7
Vanuatu, ■ *Pac. Ocean* 3 E18
Varanasi, *India* 22 C5
Värmland, □ *Swed.* 17 G12
Varna, *Bulg.* 15 C12
Västerås, *Swed.* 17 G14
Vasterbotten, □ *Norw.* 16 D14
Vasternorrland, □ *Norw.* 16 E14
Västervik, *Swed.* 17 H14
Västmanland, □ *Swed.* 17 G14
Vatnajökull, *Iceland* 16 D5
Veneto, □ *Italy* 14 B4
Venézia, □ *Italy* 14 B5
Venezuela, ■ *S. Amer.* 40 B5
Veracruz, *Mexico* 38 D5
Vereeniging, *S. Africa* 33 K5
Vermont, □ *U.S.A.* 37 B12
Verona, *Italy* 14 B4

Versailles, *France* 12 B5
Vest-Agder, □ *Norw.* 17 G9
Vesterålen, *Norw.* 16 B13
Vestfjorden, *Norw.* 16 B13
Vesuvio, *Italy* 14 D6
Viborg, *Den.* 17 H10
Vichy, *France* 12 C5
Victoria, *Australia* 27 F7
Victoria, *Canada* 34 D7
Victoria Falls, *Zimbabwe* 33 H5
Victoria I., *Canada* 34 A8
Victoria, L., *Africa* 32 E6
Vienna = Wien, *Austria* 10 D8
Vientos, Paso de los, *W. Indies* .39 C10
Vietnam, ■ *Asia* 23 B2
Vigo, *Spain* 13 A1
Vilnius, *Lithuania* 18 D3
Viña del Mar, *Chile* 42 C2
Virgin Is., *W. Indies* 39 D12
Virginia, □ *U.S.A.* 37 C11
Visby, *Swed.* 17 H15
Vitória, *Brazil* 41 H10
Vitoria, *Spain* 13 A4
Vladivostok, *Russia* 19 E14
Volga, ≈ *Russia* 18 E5
Volgograd, *Russia* 18 E5
Vólos, *Greece* 15 E10
Volta, L., *Ghana* 30 G4
Vorarlberg, □ *Austria* 10 E4
Voronezh, *Russia* 18 D4
Vyatka, *Russia* 18 D5

W

Waco, *U.S.A.* 37 D7
Wâd Medanî, *Sudan* 31 F11
Wakayama, *Japan* 24 B4
Wakefield, *U.K.* 6 D6
Wakkanai, *Japan* 24 E11
Wałbrzych, *Poland* 10 C8
Wales, □ *U.K.* 7 E4
Wallasey, *U.K.* 6 D4
Wallsend, *U.K.* 6 B6
Walney I., *U.K.* 6 C4
Walsall, *U.K.* 7 E5
Walvisbaai, *S. Africa* 33 J2
Wanganui, *N.Z.* 28 H5
Warley, *U.K.* 7 E6
Warrington, *U.K.* 6 D5
Warszawa, *Poland* 11 B10
Warwick, *U.K.* 7 E6
Warwickshire, □ *U.K.* 7 E6
Wash, The, *U.K.* 6 E8
Washington, □ *U.S.A.* 36 A2
Washington D.C., *U.S.A.* 37 C11
Waterbury, *U.S.A.* 37 B12
Waterford, *Ire.* 9 D4
Watford, *U.K.* 7 F7
Weald, The, *U.K.* 7 F7
Welkom, *S. Africa* 33 K5
Wellesley Is., *Australia* 27 B6
Wellington, *N.Z.* 28 J5
Wellington I., *Chile* 42 F2
Wenzhou, *China* 25 D7
West Bromwich, *U.K.* 7 E6
West Glamorgan, □ *U.K.* 7 F4
West Indies 39 D10
West Midlands, □ *U.K.* 7 E6
West Sussex, □ *U.K.* 7 G7
West Virginia, □ *U.S.A.* 37 C10
West Yorkshire, □ *U.K.* 6 D6
Western Australia, □ *Oceania* 26 C3
Western Is., □ *U.K.* 8 D1
Western Sahara, ■ *Africa* 30 C2
Western Samoa, ■ *Pac. Ocean* ...2 E1
Westerwald, *Ger.* 10 C3
Westmeath, □ *Ire.* 9 C4
Weston-super-Mare, *U.K.* 7 F6
Westray, *U.K.* 8 B5
Wexford, *Ire.* 9 D5
Weymouth, *U.K.* 7 G5
Whalsay, *U.K.* 8 A8
White Nile = Nîl el Abyad, ≈ *Africa* .31 E11
White Sea = Beloye More, *Russia* .18 C4
Whitehaven, *U.K.* 6 C4
Whitehorse, *Canada* 34 B6
Wichita, *U.S.A.* 37 C7
Wichita Falls, *U.S.A.* 36 D7
Wick, *U.K.* 8 C5
Wicklow, *Ire.* 9 D5
Wien, *Austria* 10 D8
Wiesbaden, *Ger.* 10 C4
Wigan, *U.K.* 6 D5
Wight, I. of, □ *U.K.* 7 G6
Wilhelmshaven, *Ger.* 10 B4
Wilmington, *U.S.A.* 37 C11
Wiltshire, □ *U.K.* 7 F6
Winchester, *U.K.* 7 F6
Windermere, *U.K.* 6 C5
Windhoek, *Namibia* 33 J3
Windsor, *U.K.* 7 F7
Windsor, *Canada* 35 D11
Windward Is., *W. Indies* 39 E12
Winnipeg, *Canada* 34 C10
Winnipeg, L., *Canada* 34 C10
Winston Salem, *U.S.A.* 37 C10
Winterthur, *Switz.* 10 E4
Wirral, The, *U.K.* 6 D4
Wisconsin, □ *U.S.A.* 37 B9

Wishaw, *U.K.* 8 F5
Włocławek, *Poland* 11 B9
Woking, *U.K.* 7 F7
Wollongong, *Australia* 27 E9
Wolverhampton, *U.K.* 7 E5
Worcester, *U.K.* 7 E5
Worcester, *U.S.A.* 37 B12
Workington, *U.K.* 6 C4
Worksop, *U.K.* 6 D6
Worms, *Ger.* 10 D4
Worthing, *U.K.* 7 G7
Wrexham, *U.K.* 6 D4
Wrocław, *Poland* 10 C8
Wuhan, *China* 25 C6
Wuhu, *China* 25 C6
Wuppertal, *Ger.* 10 C3
Würzburg, *Ger.* 10 D4
Wyoming, □ *U.S.A.* 36 B5

X

Xi'an, *China* 25 C5
Xiaguan, *China* 25 D5
Xingu, ≈ *Brazil* 41 D8
Xinjiang Uygur, □ *China* 25 B3
Xizang, □ *China* 25 C3
Xuzhou, *China* 25 C6

Y

Yakushima, *Japan* 24 D2
Yakutsk, *Russia* 19 C13
Yamagata, *Japan* 24 G11
Yaoundé, *Cameroon* 32 D2
Yaroslavl, *Russia* 18 D4
Yazd, *Iran* 21 B4
Yell, *U.K.* 8 A7
Yellow Sea, *Asia* 25 C7
Yellowknife, *Canada* 34 B8
Yellowstone National Park, *U.S.A.* .36 B4
Yemen, ■ *Asia* 21 D4
Yenisey, ≈ *Russia* 18 C9
Yeovil, *U.K.* 7 G5
Yerevan, *Armenia* 18 E5
Yining, *China* 25 B3
Yokohama, *Japan* 24 B6
Yokosuka, *Japan* 24 B6
York, *U.K.* 6 D6
Youghal, *Ire.* 9 E4
Ystad, *Swed.* 17 J12
Yucatán, □ *Mexico* 38 D7
Yugoslavia, ■ *Europe* 15 C8
Yukon, ≈ *N. Amer.* 34 B4
Yukon Territory, □ *Canada* 34 B6

Z

Zabrze, *Poland* 11 C9
Zagazig, *Egypt* 31 B11
Zagreb, *Croatia* 14 B8
Zagros Mts., *Iran* 21 B3
Zaïre, ≈ *Africa* 32 E4
Zaïre, ■ *Africa* 32 E4
Zákinthos, *Greece* 15 F9
Zambezi, ≈ *Africa* 33 H6
Zambia, ■ *Africa* 33 G5
Zamora, *Spain* 13 B3
Zanzibar, *Tanzania* 32 F7
Zaporozhye, *Ukraine* 18 E4
Zaragoza, *Spain* 13 B5
Zaria, *Nigeria* 30 F6
Zemlya Frantsa Iosifa, *Russia* ...18 B6
Zhanghua, *Taiwan* 25 D7
Zhangjiakou, *China* 25 B6
Zhengzhou, *China* 25 C6
Zhenjiang, *China* 25 C6
Zibo, *China* 25 C6
Zigong, *China* 25 D5
Zimbabwe, ■ *Africa* 33 H5
Zürich, *Switz.* 10 E4
Zwickau, *Ger.* 10 C6